FLIGHTS OF FANTASY

HEROES OF 1962 INDO-CHINA WAR, ABU TANI'S SPEAKING TREE & OTHER ARTICLES

GROUP CAPTAIN MOHONTO PANGING PAO, VAYU SENA MEDAL (RETD)

Notion Press

No.8, 3rd Cross Street,
CIT Colony, Mylapore,
Chennai, Tamil Nadu – 600004

First Published by Notion Press 2021
Copyright © Group Captain Mohonto Panging Pao,
Vayu Sena Medal (Retd) 2021
All Rights Reserved.

ISBN 978-1-63669-574-7

CONTENTS

3. Abu Tani's Speaking Tree

CONTENTS

4. Heroes of 1962 Indo-China War

5. Heroes of Arunachal & Indo-Pak Conflicts

6. Indo-China Relations, Strategy & Security Scenario

CONTENTS

7. Historical Legends

8. Evolution of Society

CONTENTS

ACKNOWLEDGEMENTS

I would like to thank many people who have contributed towards successful completion and publication of the book.

Editors and staff of Arunachal Times, Eastern Sentinel, Arunachal Review for perusing and publishing my articles.

Young artist Mingki Burang and coursemate Rajat Baijal for spending many hours with me to create the expressive caricatures.

Dr Kaling Jerang, Kingman Komut for being avid readers and critics.

My wife Dr Lung Perme Panging, family members & friends for encouraging and supporting my writings.

Finally thanks to all my readers who are the most prized for me.

Thank you all!

FOREWORD

Group Captain Mohonto Panging Pao (Retd) was an ace pilot flying the most sophisticated fighter jets before he hanged his boots and have become a writer, a columnist, an entrepreneur and a social worker, rededicating his life for the society and to the humanity. He had already established himself as a writer through his already published short story book *"Kéérook & Other Stories of North East India"*. The stories in the book narrate tales about the lives and livelihood of people of North East India. North East India is a potpourri of numerous tribes and races living together in an area intermingling with valleys, hills and rivers with each tribe and race have their own unique lifestyle, customs, traditions, language and dresses. The stories of the book are told in lucid style and poignant narratives were replete with human ethos that comes from the pen who feels other's agony as his own agony.

Group Captain Mohonto Panging Pao (Retd) has become a household name in Arunachal Pradesh through his weekly column 'Flights of Fantasy' published every Sunday in Arunachal times. He also writes articles in the Eastern Sentinel, Arunachal Review and other magazines on various topics. To speak about this book, in the first Chapter titled 'Flights of Fantasy', the articles tells the readers the thrill of knowing an unknown world of pilots who had lived a life of adventure in the unlimited horizon of blue sky vis-à-vis a state of psychology that the pilots go through while flying in a speed higher than the speed of sound in a height from where sky looks black and mind becomes blank like a flyleaf. Barring first chapter, in other chapters he has landed us on the ground to confront the reality that sizes us on day to day life with various problems right from the dilapidated road condition starting from our doorstep to threat at our border from China. With his introduction of heroes of 1962 war in the then our NEFA which he nomenclatures as 'Heroes of 1962 War in Arunachal' he was able to enthuse renewed patriotic zeal in our minds. With subtle suggestions without resorting to sermonization, he had indicated ways and mean for solving many problems of Arunachal Pradesh to those who are at the helms of affair through some of his articles. In this way the "Flights of Fantasy' contains an array of articles written for his weekly column in Arunachal Times that in my opinion will serve many purposes for which an ace pilot like Mohonto Panging Pao has taken mouse and keyboard in his hands.

I hope the readers will like it.

Itanagar

11th October, 2020

Yeshe Dorjee Thongchi

Author, Padma Shri &
Sahitya Akademi Winner

1

FLIGHTS OF FANTASY

HELLO ITANAGAR...HERE COMES THE SUKHOI...

It was a routine phone call from Headquarters that led to the event. As Chief Operations Officer at Air Force Tezpur, I received the phone call asking if we could take on the Air Force events at the Silver Jubilee Arunachal Day celebrations planned at Itanagar on 20 February 2012. I replied *'Of Course we could and it would be a flawless Show'*. Being from Arunachal Pradesh, I considered it as a lucky break that I got an opportunity to contribute to the Arunachal Day Silver Jubilee celebrations. Further inquiries revealed that we were to plan a petal drop by a helicopter and flypast by a three aircraft

Sukhoi-30 formation. I could not believe my luck and I resolved to lead the Sukhoi flypast myself.

The planning for such an event involving flying operations must start with a physical visit to the site, followed by an airborne reconnaissance from a helicopter over the area and along the planned path to be followed by the aircraft. This was required since Itanagar township covered a large area with many vertical towers and high rise buildings coming up around the township. In addition, there were many hills around the township and along the planned path of the aircraft. The layout of the venue was also important in terms of VIPs/Dais/Audience facing direction vís-a-vís direction of the flypast for maximum appeal to the audience.

The next day, I visited Itanagar in a helicopter. We carried hand held Global Positioning System (GPS) sets, binoculars, handycam and large scale maps of the area. After a meeting with the Organising Party including the Chief Organiser, DC and SP, we visited the actual site of the event i.e. Indira Gandhi Park at Itanagar. After studying the actual site, we decided to set up a Control Centre for coordinating the flypast from the ground in terms of coinciding the flypast exactly with the planned event and for safety in terms of bird activity in the area. In this case the fighter flypast was planned to fly past the dais for the first time at the moment of the Chief Guest declaring the Arunachal Day celebrations *Open*.

The detailed planning for the flypast was carried out by the young pilots. We carried out a detailed briefing for the flypast and decided four Sukhoi-30MKI fighter aircraft for the flypast; three aircraft carrying out the main flypast with one aircraft as a standby. We also decided to carry out one practice run on 18 February keeping the timings same. We planned to carry out one four minute orbit at a point north of Behali in Assam. This was required to cater for any change of timings. After the orbit, the plan was to head for the Initial Point (IP). The IP was a point in the valley south west of Itanagar about 30 km away. The timings were worked backwards from the planned time over the dais up to the final second. From the IP it was a straight run in on a north easterly heading of 2 minutes flying time at 900 km/h till the dais. The first flypast was planned to be a level flypast. The first flypast would be followed by a second flypast after 10 minutes. The second flypast would end with all three Sukhoi-30MKI aircraft peeling off abeam the dais to execute a Trishul manoeuvre. The practice on 18 February went off as planned.

On 20 February 2012, the four Sukhoi-30MKI aircraft got airborne on time. Flying at 800 km/h the 65 odd kilometres to the Orbit Point at Behali was covered in about 5 min. The formation carried out one orbit at the Orbit Point as planned. Radio contact with flypast control set up at the dais revealed minor changes in the time abeam the dais due to changes in the parade timings. Once cleared by flypast control to set course, the formation set course for the IP and started descending to lower heights negotiating the hills in the area. Over the IP the formation turned towards Indira Gandhi Park on a north easterly heading. Over the IP the fourth aircraft peeled off to return back to base. As the formation descended to lower heights within the narrow valley, the two aircraft on the wings of the leader (wingmen) started closing in to get into close formation. As the lead aircraft, I kept a sharp look out for birds, other obstructions like high tension cables, towers etc while accelerating to a speed of 900 km/h to make good exact time in seconds abeam the dais. As the formation approached Indira Gandhi Park, as planned, we picked up the Chief Minister's bungalow and quickly aligned with the planned point abeam the dais. As we crossed the Chief Minister's bungalow, the Indira Gandhi Park quickly appeared in front and the formation roared past the dais in just 5 seconds!

For the second run, the formation turned around Naharlagun, Banderdewa and returned back to the IP. From the IP the formation repeated the same run in procedure towards the point abeam the dais. This time at a pre-selected point, 1 km short of the dais, on my call on the radio, the formation executed the Trishul manoeuvre. Both wingmen turned outwards by 30 degree and pitched up engaging afterburners. As the leader, I pitched up the aircraft vertically up, engaged afterburners and executed a vertical roll. Having executed the manoeuvre, on my call on radio, the formation joined up again and set course back to base. The formation landed back at base within the next 10 min.

We came to know later that the Sukhoi-30 formation created a big buzz at the event during the two fly pasts. The loud jet sounds created by the three Sukhoi-30 aircraft were ear splitting and deafening. It was a spectacular show indeed and was appreciated by all spectators since this was the first occasion wherein fighter aircraft had flown at low levels over Itanagar and carried out manoeuvres. A special honour for me was courtesy *Eastern Sentinel* which carried a big front page story with photographs on the same day. More than anything else, hailing from Arunachal Pradesh, it was indeed an honour for me to perform over the capital of our great state. Maybe someday in the future, another Arunachali will repeat the performance.

ITANAGAR TO PASIGHAT IN 15 MINUTES...

Our squadron was tasked to undertake a routine mission over areas covering Arunachal Pradesh. I was the Commanding Officer of the Sukhoi-30MKI Squadron. The officer in charge of planning the flying did me a favour and planned me as the leader of the two aircraft formation. The mission was planned to fly over Guwahati, Tezpur, Itanagar, Ziro, Daporijo, Aalo and Pasighat before returning to base via Dibrugarh. Since the mission duration was longish we were planned to refuel once in the air from a tanker aircraft.

The two aircraft got airborne on time. We climbed to the cruise height of 9 km and contacted the civil and military agencies enroute on radio. Cleared by all concerned agencies we set course towards the target area maintaining a cruising speed of 900 km/h. As planned, we carried out the rendezvous with the tanker aircraft ahead of Guwahati. Matching speeds with the tanker aircraft we joined up and flew alongside the tanker aircraft. The tanker aircraft reeled out the refuelling drogues and baskets. After being cleared by the tanker aircraft, both fighter aircraft connected & coupled with the drogues and baskets with precision. After the successful coupling, both fighters tanked up and took in about 6 tons of fuel each. Both the fighter aircraft detached after the aerial refuelling. The process of refuelling was over in about ten minutes.

After the aerial refuelling, the two fighter aircraft headed towards Itanagar. The Assam valley is a relatively narrow valley with the valley width varying from about thirty kilometres at the narrowest to about 100 kilometres at the widest. The valley is surrounded by the Himalayas in the north and east with the Patkai hill ranges in the south. The valley is dominated by the mighty Brahmaputra River flowing along the middle of the valley. After crossing Kameng or Jia Bhoroli river our path towards Itanagar passed north of Biswanath Charali and Hollongi. Towards Itanagar, the formation descended to about 4 km height. Itanagar township has grown into a large township over the years and can be picked up from large distances. The township is spread out mostly along a south west - north east axis almost along our approach direction. Despite the high speeds, at Itanagar we picked up Raj Bhawan helipad, Indira Gandhi Park and the Chief Minister's Bungalow. We carried out an orbit over Itanagar at the same height keeping clear of the hills.

After the orbit, we set course for Ziro on a north easterly heading. We maintained a comfortable height maintaining adequate safety above the hills. On the path towards Ziro, we kept Naharlagun and Yupia on the right. We picked up the Ranganadi Hydro Power Project on the right, almost overflew Yazali before spotting Hapoli and the Ziro airstrip. We covered the distance from Itanagar to Ziro in under 4 minutes. Ziro valley appeared beautiful from the air with pine and fir trees surrounding the valley. From Ziro, the formation headed for Daporijo. The path to Daporijo passed north of Raga township. We approached Daporijo from the valley on the south west which led to the township. Daporijo is situated on the western bank of the Subansiri river at a junction of three narrow valleys. From Ziro it took us less than 4 minutes to reach Daporijo. We picked up the airstrip and Daporijo Bazaar. Overhead Daporijo the formation turned right crossed the Subansiri river, kept Dumporijo township to the right and headed for Aalo. Towards Aalo we spotted Basar township about 15 km to our right. It took the formation about 4 minutes to reach Aalo. Aalo township is spread out in a north - south axis, is situated on the southern bank of the Siyom river and we picked up the airstrip and the bazaar area.

From Aalo we turned further right and set course for Pasighat. The formation increased speed to 1000 km/h and headed for Pasighat keeping the Siang river on the left. Enroute we picked up Pangin and Renging to our left. We spotted Pasighat within 3 minutes of leaving Aalo. Pasighat is located close to the confluence of the Siang and Siku rivers. The plains start from Pasighat and the mighty Siang river starts widening at Pasighat. The oldest town of Pasighat looked lovely from the air with the Siang spreading out into many branches like the tentacles of a Hydra. We carried out an orbit over Pasighat and picked up the airstrip, bazaar, JN College, Ranaghat bridge, Mebo township and other areas. After the orbit the formation set course for Dibrugarh via Namsing village and further back to base.

It was an exhilarating experience to fly over Arunachal Pradesh. As a child I had visited or stayed at all these townships. During my young days, Pasighat town was one day walking from our village and I have walked this route many times. In this mission we had covered the distance from Itanagar to Pasighat via Ziro, Daporijo and Aalo in just about 15 min. This time was achieved maintaining average cruise speeds and without going supersonic. There is a perspective difference between views from the ground and from the air. Aerial views of Arunachal Pradesh are indeed very rare. But when you get an opportunity, it is worth its weight in gold. Arunachal Pradesh is beautiful from the air! To paraphrase the comment by India's first Cosmonaut Wing Commander Rakesh Sharma (Retd), from the air Arunachal Pradesh appears *'Saare Jahan Se Achcha'!*

Eject…Eject…Eject…

It was my fourth solo sortie on the Hunter fighter aircraft. We were flying at a height of 20,000 feet positioning for some aerobatic manoeuvres. The sky was crystal clear and the earth seemed far away. The Kasai river below appeared like a long slender serpent crawling across the lush green paddy fields. Puffs of smoke were visible from the numerous brick kilns and chimneys of the small factories dotting the country side. The pattern of paddy fields appeared as a vast mesh of squares and rectangles. The numerous villages seemed as a distant collection of tiny building blocks. The only evidence of flying was the slow movement of the earth and the dials indicating the various parameters. The monotonous buzz in the cockpit was intermittently broken by the static of the periodic radio transmissions. The sheer joy of flying was unmatched and only those privileged few could sense the joy and elation of solo flying in the sky. If there could be a heaven on earth, this was it. The absolute sense of freedom, separated from the earthly living, made possible a utopian dream to be fulfilled only by aviators. Your own fate and destiny now lay in your own skills of manoeuvring the ten ton machine in the sky.

I put the Hunter aircraft in a dive. All the dials indicated that the Hunter was behaving like the 'fair lady' she was supposed to be. It is then that I heard an unfamiliar sound and saw the dials winding down crazily. I instinctively pushed the throttle forward. But the dials kept winding down. That is when I realised that it was a case of engine failure. I went into denial mode. How could an engine failure occur when everything was perfectly normal till now? But the dials kept winding down and I went into a state of shock. The numerous dials I was trained to read at a glance vanished right in front of my eyes and my brain was suddenly spinning around. Time seemed to have stopped with eternity setting in.

After a few eternal seconds, I snapped out of this state of shock like being awakened from a long sweet dream. A serene calmness now set in and I got into the task of tackling the emergency at hand. Recovered from the shock state, I could read the dials now and I saw the speed was 150 knots. I pushed the joystick forward and put the Hunter aircraft in a glide towards base. I called out on the radio that I had an engine failure in the air. I decided to attempt re-starting the aero engine. My life now depended on the success of the engine restarting in the air. I attempted three relights in the air to re-start the engine. But the engine did not start. I was descending below 15000 feet and was about 50 km from base. To add to my troubles the fire warning light came on after the third attempted relight.

I informed base on the radio that I also had a 'Fire warning light' in the cockpit indicating the presence of fire in the stricken aircraft. The emergency situation was worsening in the cockpit with many systems failing and the engine not relighting with the fire warning light. I was so busy tackling the emergency at hand that there was no time to think of anyone, not even my parents back at home and God! They were pushed into the background.

I decided that it was time to leave the stricken aircraft and informed base on the radio that I would be carrying out an Ejection. The thought of ejection reminded me of the ejection just six months earlier when the pilot lost his life as the parachute did not open in the air. Then I saw the twin towns of Kharagpur and Midnapur straight ahead in our path. I informed base on the radio that I would be turning right away from the twin towns and ejecting. By then we were at 9000 feet height. So many pilots had lost their lives due to late ejections or not ejecting at all. For the pilot, up in the sky, the cockpit was a comfortable home away from home. Sitting in the cockpit with hundreds of switches and dials around him for hours together put the pilot at total ease. It was almost as if man and machine are bonded together in time and space.

I grasped the ejection handle above my head with both hands, straightened out my sitting posture and pulled the ejection handle without hesitation. Time seemed to move in slow motion. Something was pushing me from below my seat. The rockets underneath the seat had fired and the myriad sequence of automatic ejection procedure in split seconds precision had been activated. I saw the glass canopy on top flying off and felt the rush of cold air hitting my body. I was being thrown out of the Hunter aircraft at a speed of 100 feet per second exposing my body to forces equivalent to 30 times the body weight. At this stage I blacked out and tumbled through the air.

When I came to his senses, I found myself floating in the air with the cool air breezing past my body. I looked up and saw the multi coloured canopy of the parachute. The parachute was swaying wildly as the wind was strong. I held the straps of the parachute tightly fearing the parachute would give way. I saw the distant earth and the thought of landing suddenly filled me with panic. I heard the distant noise of people shouting below me. I looked down and saw tiny specks of people running in my direction. I saw the black smoke from the debris of the crashed aircraft not far away. The wind was pushing me towards the aircraft crash site. The thought of the local people below harming me flashed through my mind. My survival instincts took over and I immediately made a plan to run away from the area after landing. I saw many small ponds below me. I was not sure whether I would land on water or land. Both situations demanded different procedures to land. I could not be sure and started planning my landing process for both situations.

At height, the surroundings appeared serene and beautiful. But as I fell towards earth and came closer to the ground, I found the earth rushing up to meet me. The thought of the fall fracturing my limbs flashed in my mind. And then there was no time. I banged into a muddy paddy field and fell on my back. After falling, I operated the quick release fitment to release the parachute. To my surprise the mud in the paddy field had cushioned my landing and my legs were intact. My plans of fleeing the area came to a grinding halt as I found myself surrounded by hundreds of local villagers. My survival instincts again took over.

"My mother is Bengali" I instinctively blurted out in the little Bengali I knew, since the locals were all Bengalis. Thereafter a few villagers formed a human circle around me holding hands. A hand fan appeared and one local started fanning me.

"Do you want water?" a local asked in Bengali.

"Yes" I replied sitting down on the ground. There was no time to notice the gash on my chest with slight amount of blood oozing out. The gash was caused by the zippers of my flying overall.

I kept sitting there on the ground pondering about the situation I was in. Time seemed to have frozen and everything appeared to be moving very slowly. I waited on the ground for about fifteen minutes. Due the Time Expansion, I felt that period as one hour. Soon we could hear the sound of the rescue helicopter. I stood up and started walking towards the helicopter. The rescue helicopter landed about twenty metres from me. The helicopter kept its motors running and I immediately got into the chopper. Fearing some hostile action from the locals, the helicopter immediately got airborne. A doctor examined me in the chopper.

As the chopper approached base, I saw a large gathering waiting to receive me. After a pilot ejects, the most crucial part was the arrival of the rescue helicopter. For one did not know whether the fractured body or the dead body would arrive. I noticed the entire station top brass, my course mates and instructors among those waiting for me. As the helicopter landed, I was taken to the waiting ambulance in a stretcher. I was then taken to the base hospital for the routine medical examination post ejection consisting of X-Rays and the other mandatory checks. In the hospital, a set of ten X-Rays were taken. A general surgeon examined me from head to toe and found me okay. I was then wheeled into the officer's ward and propped up on the bed. As the doctors and nurses left, the visitors started pouring in. They comprised of senior officers, my colleagues, my juniors and their families. Some came with flower bouquets, others with get well cards and eatables. My colleagues brought a birthday cake. All of them congratulated me for my new 'Birthday'. A successful ejection was considered a new life for a pilot.

Those who could not make it in the afternoon visited me in the evening and night. I sat propped up on bed all through the afternoon, evening and night. The last visitor departed at ten in the night. The officer's ward was suddenly quiet. After I was alone in the ward, the severity of the situation hit me. I shuddered thinking of what I had gone through in the day. I could have suffered from multiple fractures, cuts and bruises or perhaps would have been dead. The tension in my body being exposed to about 30 'g' was now creeping in. Till now I did not feel it in the din of all attention and affection showered on me throughout the day. I shuddered again with the thought of difference between life and death. Death had come so close. It was indeed a new birthday for me!

Fighter Flying.... Experiences Beyond Normal Life

Have you experienced Time Contraction, Time Expansion or your life span flashing in split seconds in your eyes...? Have you always seen good dreams? Do you know that dreams last for three seconds...yes, yes...three seconds only? Being fully conscious and with your eyes wide open have you experienced complete Black Out? Being fully conscious and with your eyes wide open have you experienced complete Red Out? Have you travelled faster than your own voice? Fighter Pilots experience all these and much more...!!!

All things on earth are subjected to the pull of earth's gravity. Our weights are due the earth's gravity and these conditions are termed to be under 1 g. Due to the high manoeuvrability of fighter aircraft, pilots and aircraft are routinely subjected to higher 'g' forces due to centripetal-centrifugal forces. To take an example, if one's normal weight is 60 kg, at 2 'g' the weight is doubled to 120 kg. Similarly at 3 'g' the weight is tripled to 180 kg. Present day fighter aircraft routinely manoeuvre at 5 to 6 'g' and frequently touches 8 to 9 'g'. Taking the same example, at 9 'g' the weight would be 540 kg! At 9 'g' even the 10 kg hand would be 90 kg and you would require extra powerful arms to lift your own hand! With the aircraft manoeuvring at higher 'g' forces, blood starts travelling downwards towards the lower parts of the body. If 5 to 6 'g' is sustained for prolonged periods, due to lack of blood in the eyes, the peripheral vision starts reducing and the pilot starts seeing everything in a greyish shade. This is termed as Grey Out. If the high 'g' is sustained beyond this limit for prolonged periods, due to lack of blood in the eyes, with eyes fully open and being fully conscious, the pilot sees only black. This is termed as Black Out.

Beyond Black Out, if the high 'g' is sustained for prolonged periods, due to lack of blood in the brain, the pilot becomes unconscious. The scientific term for this is G-induced Loss of Consciousness or G-LOC. It is under conditions of G-LOC that pilots see their best dreams. Unlike dreams seen while sleeping, the dreams seen during G-LOC are always good dreams; nightmares or bad dreams are never seen. Fighter pilots are trained in high speed centrifuges to practice Anti 'g' Manoeuvres and avoid getting into G-LOC. These training sessions are video graphed and retained for future de-briefs. During these training sessions many pilots experience Grey Out, Black Out and G-LOC. The videos of pilots experiencing G-LOC at centrifuges and subsequent debriefs have revealed that these dreams lasted for three seconds only! This also implies that most dreams experienced by us while sleeping that appear to be many minutes or hours long are just three seconds long! Are these not instances of Time Expansion?

The experiences explained above are under positive 'g' conditions when the weight increases. The opposite occurs under negative 'g' conditions. When a pilot experiences negative 'g', blood starts flowing upwards towards the head. When a pilot experiences prolonged minus 2 to minus 3 'g', blood is flooded into the eyes and the pilot starts seeing Red. This is termed as Red Out. Human beings tolerance to negative 'g' is much less as compared to positive 'g' tolerance.

Fighter flying is dangerous by design and attitude; it involves multiple risks associated with high manoeuvrability at extremely high speeds. People consider Formula One dangerous. The highest speeds of Formula One cars are about 300 km/h. Fighter aircraft take off at this speed! Fighter aircraft routinely fly at triple that speed at 900 km/h and regularly fly at two times the speed of sound at about 2300-2400 km/h! Under such high speed situations pilots occasionally face sudden emergency situations. Loss of an engine in the air, sudden loss of pressurisation, collision with birds in the air, occurrence of fire on parts of the aircraft, sudden loss of controllability of the aircraft, ejection from an aircraft etc may comprise of sudden emergency situations. Many pilots experience shock at the moment of occurrence of such sudden life threatening emergency situations, especially in the initial stages of career. It is under these sudden life threatening emergency situations that pilots experience numbness with shock, Time Expansion and

Time Contraction. Time passes very slowly. Five minutes is experienced as half an hour. Ten minutes is experienced as one hour. On the contrary, in Time Contraction, the pilot remains in shock as the clock ticks by.

When faced with some sudden life threatening emergency situations wherein death stares at your face, some pilots have experienced their whole life flashing in a split second in front of their eyes. It is like seeing your own life's major events and major people known to you in cinematic screening mode flashing in front of your eyes in micro seconds.

There are many other extraordinary phenomena experienced during fighter flying. Once you get airborne and the wheels are retracted, one is overwhelmed with the feeling of raw power and seamless freedom (there are no roads in the air!). The feeling of raw power with total control of a 40 ton muscular beast with 25 tons of engine power and tremendous firepower on your finger tips... what could be more filled with testosterone? It is difficult to beat the sheer thrill of high speed flying with the earth's surface zipping past you when flying very close to the surface of the earth. The unique feeling of loneliness and aloofness experienced when flying in a single cockpit fighter aircraft during dark nights over the desolate desert... the claustrophobic feeling of flying into a huge, black wall when flying during dark nights over the oceans under overcast skies. Spectacular views of *Halo and Corona* around the Sun and Moon during unique cloudy days and nights can be witnessed during flying.

When flying at the end of the troposphere at about 17-18 km height, the earth starts appearing round and the sky colour starts turning blackish. At this height, the high speeds are not appreciated as the earth moves past slowly and stronger sun rays hit you due to the rarefied atmosphere. If there was sufficient fuel, a pilot could chase the Sun and not allow it to set! With most weather phenomena restricted to the lower troposphere, most fighter pilots are able to penetrate and fly above weather. Once above the weather, beautiful blue skies may be seen totally removed from the earth covered under a blanket of clouds. During the process, there is the added experience of flying through the cloudy mixture of air and water. On today's highly manoeuvrable fighter aircraft one could carry out manoeuvres previously considered impossible. Various aerobatic manoeuvres like looping manoeuvres, rolling manoeuvres, flying inverted (you hang on the straps), vertical climbs and dives are routinely practiced. Today advanced manoeuvres like Tail Slides (moving backwards), Yaw Turns (Turning on own axes like a helicopter), Somersault etc are also regularly practiced. Have you seen birds executing these manoeuvres?

Like any other profession, fighter flying has its own advantages and disadvantages. It is not easy to become a good fighter pilot, but it is not too difficult also. Only birds were designed to fly. Human beings are not birds. But today human beings are beating birds at their own game! As explained earlier, there are many 'out of normal life' phenomena that can be experienced during fighter flying only. It may not be wrong to summarise and say that 'Fighter Flying is Different'! Do any of you want to fly fighter aircraft?

Dreams Unlimited

Everyone sees Dreams. Dreams are explained as a succession of images, ideas, emotions and sensations that usually occur involuntarily in the mind during certain stages of sleep. The content and purpose of dreams are not fully understood, although they have been a topic of scientific, philosophical and religious interest throughout history. As per Hindu Scriptures, dream is one of three states that the soul experiences during its lifetime, the other two states being the Waking State and the Sleeping State. Even in our tribal customs many of our priests and elders draw meaning from dreams. Many people even plan or cancel events based on dreams!

Dreams occur mainly during the rapid-eye movement (REM) stage of sleep, when brain activity is high and resembles that of being awake. It is reported that the length of dreams can vary from a few seconds to approximately 20 - 30 minutes. It is also reported that the average person has three to five dreams per night; however, most dreams are quickly forgotten. During a typical lifespan, based on these figures, an average person could spend a total of about six years dreaming only! Opinions about the meaning of dreams have varied and shifted through time and culture. Many endorse the theory of Sigmund Freud - that dreams reveal insight into hidden desires and emotions. Many say that dreams are based on random events.

Some of the best dreams in life are experienced when flying fighter aircraft. When fighter pilots carry out extreme manoeuvres their bodies are stressed due to centripetal/ centrifugal forces subjecting their bodies to very high 'g' forces. All matter on earth is affected by gravity which is normally considered 1 'g'. Fighter aircraft routinely manoeuvre at 5-6 'g' going up to 9 'g'. While manoeuvring at high 'g' forces, blood is drained downwards from head towards the feet. This leads to lack of blood in the eyes and brain finally leading to a semi-conscious state called G-Induced Loss of Consciousness or

G-LOC. It is during this semi-conscious state that dreams are seen during fighter flying. Most fighter pilots experience these dreams during their flying careers. To expose fighter pilots to high 'g' situations, they undergo indoctrination training at specially built centrifuges which are rotated at very high speeds to simulate High 'g' forces. The entire sequences of events are recorded by specially built cameras and videos. It is seen and recorded during these training sessions that dreams last for 3 Seconds only. These 3 Seconds are felt like eternity during dreams!

There are also other types of dreams like Day Dreaming, Hallucinations, Dream Walking and Nightmares! Common citizens also see slightly different form of dreams. They see dreams of employment, development, free education, free medical care, good roads, 24 x 7 stabilised electricity, peace & stability etc. Like it is difficult to realise dreams seen in our sleep, it appears that many of these dreams of common citizens are also difficult to achieve!

To paraphrase former President Late APJ Abdul Kalam who said "Dreams are not those that we see while sleeping...Dreams are those that don't let us sleep"!

By the way in which Language of do you see dreams? Is there a language of mental waves?

Arunachal Pradesh: New Bermuda Triangle?

On 3 June 2019, an An-32 aircraft of the Indian Air Force (IAF) on a routine flight from Jorhat in Assam to Mechuka in Shi Yomi district of Arunachal Pradesh, with 13 personnel on board, vanished somewhere between Aalo and Mechuka. A massive search operation, including aircraft, satellites, army, police and local villagers, is ongoing to locate the aircraft's crash site. Research reveals that there have been too many aircraft crashes in Arunachal Pradesh. Since 1995, 13 aircraft have crashed in Arunachal, claiming 106 lives. Among the crashed aircraft are 10 helicopters, two An-32 aircraft and one Sukhoi-30MKI aircraft. During the last 10 years there has been an average of one aircraft crash per year, claiming 70 lives, making an average of nine lives lost per year. Another worrying matter is that the majority of these crashes have been in the Tawang area. Many prominent lives have been lost in these crashes, including that of a sitting Chief Minister, a cabinet minister, a union minister, and senior officials.

With so many crashes occurring in the state, many are asking if Arunachal is the new Bermuda Triangle? It is said that a number of aircraft and ships have disappeared under mysterious circumstances in the Bermuda Triangle located somewhere in the Atlantic ocean. There are many reasons for these aircraft crashes in Arunachal. The foremost reason is bad weather. It is widely known that weather in mountainous Arunachal is very fickle and turns into bad weather quickly. Despite the knowledge of the fickle weather conditions, most of the aircraft operating in our area are not configured with the standard equipment required for bad weather flying like the terrain collision avoidance system, the ground proximity warning system etc.

The other factor causing these accidents is pilot error. Despite the knowledge of bad and fickle weather, pilots take chances to penetrate bad weather in the mountains, leading to a crash. We require very mature pilots operating in Arunachal Pradesh. Another aspect is the lack of essential services like fire tenders, and poorly maintained helipads and airports.

There is need for stricter control on aviation in our area, in the form of Standard Operating Procedures (SOP) and laying down weather criteria for flying. For enforcing these SOPs and exercising strict control over aviation, we require professionally qualified aviators to control aviation in our area. Most officials of the civil aviation department have no idea about aviation.

Many days of search are undertaken to locate crash sites. There is a piece of equipment called the Emergency Locator Transmitter (ELT), which is automatically activated in case of a crash. The activated signals are picked up by satellites and the position of the crash site is displayed. The question is, even in the modern era, why were none of these crashed aircraft equipped with ELT?

Civil aviation is poised to increase following the operationalization of the airports in Pasighat, Tezu, Mechuka, Ziro, etc. If these urgent steps are not taken, we may see more aircraft crashes and loss of precious lives. It's high time we removed this tag of Arunachal being called the new Bermuda Triangle.

2

HAMARA ARUNACHAL

HAMARA ARUNACHAL..!

HAMARA ARUNACHAL...Arunachal Pradesh...the Land of the Rising Sun...the Pradesh of *14th century Malinithan*, the *medieval Ita Fort*, the land of *Parsuram Kund* of Mahabharat era where *Parsuram* washed away his sins, the land of *Bhismaknagar* and the beautiful *Rukmini* who was whisked away in marriage by Lord Krishna...the land of the 400 years old *second largest monastery* of the Buddhists.

HAMARA ARUNACHAL... the Pradesh of picturesque Mechuka, scenic Ziro valley, lovely landscape of Bomdila, Dirang, Tawang...snow laden Mayudia...white water rafting on the Siang, Subansiri and Dibang rivers, challenge of fresh water angling in Kameng, Siang, Dibang and Lohit rivers... rejuvenating mountain trekking in the virgin areas of Pemako...

HAMARA ARUNACHAL...the Pradesh of 28 major tribes, 100 sub tribes, 50 distinct languages and dialects...intermingling and happily living alongside each other for centuries in complete harmony with people and nature...Animists, Buddhists, Hindus, Christians living peacefully...

HAMARA ARUNACHAL...the largest state in North East India...with the lowest density of population in the country...the Pradesh of the majestic Hornbill, exotic orchids, rare animal and bird species...

HAMARA ARUNACHAL...the Pradesh of hardworking, sturdy tribal villagers who tend to be brutally honest, display high integrity, helpful out of the way...one rarely heard of rape, murder, burglary in tribal villages in the olden days...

HAMARA ARUNACHAL...also the Pradesh of big and expensive SUVs, many rich politicians, contractors, government officials...many multi-millionaires... maybe one of the highest density of them vis-á-vis the population...

HAMARA ARUNACHAL...also dependant on aid from central government... only few industries in the state due to inadequate electricity supply, poor roads, unavailability of raw material...a nascent tourism industry due to poor infrastructure, transportation, roads, bleak electricity...

HAMARA ARUNACHAL...also a Pradesh with pot holed roads in almost all district head quarters and capital, frequent electricity load shedding...very low voltage...water scarcity despite numerous rivers...

HAMARA ARUNACHAL...also with people who erect structures and plantations overnight to claim land compensation...people oppose dams, airfields, railways, colleges...just about everything!

HAMARA ARUNACHAL...also a Pradesh with too many *Unions and Organisations* ...there seems to all kinds of them including an *Unemployed Engineers Association..*!

HAMARA ARUNACHAL...also land of *Khushi-Khushi*...land of bandhs!

HAMARA ARUNACHAL...ya...KISKA ARUNACHAL?

MIND YOUR LANGUAGE...!

What is your mobile number? My mobile number is *Nine Por Tree Sik Zero Pipe Pipe Por Por Zero*...this is how many of us will pronounce 9436055440...!!

Belonging to the Tibeto-Burman stock, most of the native people from North East India have typical vocabulary, intonation and pronunciation traits. These typical traits could be due to usage over hundreds of years and maybe some genetics also! There are many words and pronunciations typically used in this area only. Pronunciations/words like *Ng..,Ngo.., Nyi..., é, í*...are typical to this area. Names like Phongwasun Ngamgadam, Thangwagam Lowangading, Mewlai Tingakhatra etc appears as tongue twisters to other Indians....just as Chinnadorai Subramanian, Elangovan Namboodripad, Mulayilthara Sadasivan are tongue twisters to us!!

Most mainlanders would pronounce the name *Míbang* as Meebang or Mibang...*Émul* would be pronounced as Eemul or Imul...*Ména* would be called Mina or Meena...*Ngo* would be pronounced as *No*...*Donyi* would be pronounced as *Doni*....*Nyodu* would be called *Nodu*...*Nyago* as *Nago*...!

Likewise most natives cannot pronounce certain syllables and pronunciations. Think would be called *Tink*...Four would be called *Por*... Five would be called *Pipe*...Six would be called *Sik*...!! Hindi words like *Accha* would be called *Assa*...*Bhindi* would be called *Bindi*...*Chhuri* would be called *Suri* etc. There is difficulty in pronouncing words/syllables with requirement to roll the tongue with the upper mouth...!!

Then there is this Assamese connection with older names and words. *a...is pronounced like an o....Arati or Aarti is Aroti...Anima is Onima...Bharati is Bharoti...etc. Roti is called Ruti...*

There are typically words prevalent in North East due to usage....*Bitter Gourd* is called *Kerala* instead of *Karela*...Kerala is a State of India!!...*Brinjal* or *Baygan* is called *Baygun*...In entire East India, *Samosa* is called *Singhara*... *Mungphali (Ground nuts)* is called *Badam*...!

When the Hindi teacher taught *"Ka Kha Ga Gha Nga...."*...the native student repeated *"Ka Ka Ga Ga Nga..."*....the teacher scolded the student... however the issue was the student could not pronounce *kha* and *gha*...!!

With many students studying outside the region and with wide proliferation of Hindi movies and Hindi TV Channels, pronunciation is improving. Occasionally one can hear native comperes/emcees and announcers using correct pronunciations of both English and Hindi languages. Otherwise listening to speeches in Hindi by our leaders are a hilarious experience!!

With improvements in pronunciation, shopkeepers will not give you *Bindi* when you ask for *Bhindi*...and we will not be eating *Kerala and Baygun*...!!

Spicy and Bland…!

Most native people of North East India like their food as simple and bland. A meal generally comprises of boiled rice, boiled meat/fish with green vegetables and chillies/salt. Generally the only spice components are locally grown ginger, garlic and fermented bamboo shoot.

Till rice was introduced, our food comprised of millets, maize, tree extracts and leafy green vegetables extracted from the jungle. Many types of

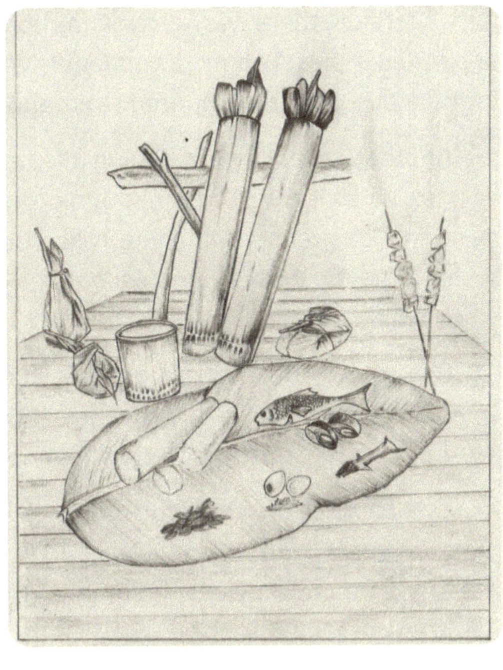

vegetables were extracted from the forest and many of them are still considered delicacies. In the absence of major spices many plants extracted from the jungle were used to spice up the food due to the tangy and pungent flavours.

Many roots are also eaten. The roots comprise of Yam or Sweet potato, Tapioca or Casava, Colocasia or Arum. Roots are baked in fire ash or simply boiled and consumed. After the introduction of rice, it replaced most forms of millets and maize as the staple diet.

Another favourite is Bamboo Shoot. Tender bamboo shoots are extracted and consumed in different forms. It could be consumed in raw tender form or fermented and consumed in different forms with sour and tangy tastes.

Meat and fish are procured from the forest/rivers. In addition to consumption of fresh meat, meat/fish are smoked on fire and preserved for consumption later. Meat/fish are also grilled or baked. Fowls and pigs were traditionally domesticated and reared for consumption. *Mithuns* were reared for consumption during special occasions and festivals. Goats and cattle were introduced later as sources of meat.

Another tribal delicacy is fermented soya beans. Fermented soya beans are mixed with salt and chillies for a pungent and tangy flavour.

Many types of fruits are also domestically grown for consumption. Fruits like berries, papaya, mango, jackfruit, oranges, apple, kiwi and bananas are readily available. Many other wilds berries and fruits are also extracted from the jungle and consumed.

Traditionally, most native people were not exposed to wheat, lentils and milk. Therefore there was no consumption of wheat products like *bread, roti or paratha*. Wheat products and lentils were introduced later. Similarly the introduction of cattle brought in milk and it's by products.

Another aspect is the timing of meals. As traditionally practiced in villages, lunch is eaten early in the morning followed by dinner early in the evening just after sunset. There is no concept of breakfast! Like the tribal saying "One must eat a full meal at the start of the day...since it is not sure when would be the next meal"!

One more aspect is the universal liking for chillies. With age, the taste buds shift towards more bitter, tangy and pungent tastes! It is common for aged people to demand bitter and pungent items during occasions.

To add spice to taste buds, one of most common items chewed by most natives is *Paan* with *betel nut* and *lime*. Many people add tobacco and tree barks for more 'Kick'! It is common to find many villagers with reddish mouths with typical Paan smells!

Like our simple and bland meals, native villagers were also simple, honest and trustworthy. With the introduction of different spices in our food, our lives have also become spicy and complicated!! It appears that we have spiced up our food and lives...!!!

LAUGHTER THE BEST MEDICINE...!

Why are we so serious in life? It seems that everyone is so busy with their lives that there is no time to laugh! In govt jobs or in MNCs/PSUs any one laughing is considered to be wasting time or displaying casual attitude. At work, one is supposed to keep working with a grim face. An effective boss is stiff collared, not supposed to smile and be stern always.

In many of our houses we rarely laugh or joke. When we meet in gatherings in villages or towns also we hardly joke or laugh. We are so serious that even husband and wife do not walk together. Husband walks ahead with the wife following behind by few paces! Similarly in offices also, we are too serious for any laughter or jokes. We are too serious in our towns, villages, families, offices, schools.

In our tribal society there are too many *Kebangs/Kebaa/Mels* going on in our villages and towns. *Kebangs/Kebaa/Mels* are conducted for resolving property disputes, land disputes, marital disputes, petty crimes, violence etc. Another new addition to this list of disputes is defamation cases. It is estimated that there are hundreds of *Kebangs/ Kebaa/ Mels* going on per day in our villages and towns! In many cases, even when the disputes are being tried in judicial courts, *Kebangs/Kebaa/Mels* are held for the same. Despite so many *Kebangs/ Kebaa/ Mels* the peace index in society seems to be going down!

The rare jokes are at the cost of another person, tribe or organization. We do not have the ability to laugh at ourselves (Remember *Sardarji jokes*). If anyone pulls a pun on us individually, our tribe or our political party or our organization, we take it too seriously and are ready for another *Kebang/ Kebaa/Mel!* Reaction to many disputes are typically *'Kaat Dunga'* or *'Maar Dunga'* or *'Dao Dekha Hai...?'*

Due to our seriousness in life, stress levels are increasing, leading to lifestyle diseases like high Blood Pressure, Hypertension, Diabetes etc. Due to high stress levels, most of us are always short tempered, irritable and argumentative. We are always in a rush, always over speeding and overtaking; we want to arrive last and jump the line. We are irritable, rude and start the day shouting at each other!

As per many studies, laughter has many benefits. Laughter relaxes the body, boosts immunity, combats depression, relieves pain and may help us live longer. Laughter triggers the release of endorphins, the body's natural feel-good chemicals. Endorphins promote an overall sense of well-being and relieve pain. Considering the positive effects of laughter, many Laughter Clubs are operating in many cities and towns. Shows like 'Comedy Nights with Kapil Sharma' and 'The Great Indian Laughter Challenge' are gaining popularity across the country.

Is being too serious in life making us rich or bringing about development overnight? At least being little bit *Bindass* and amusing can make our mundane lives easier to live, make us healthier leading to a more peaceful and healthier society. Let's start the day with a Laughter Pill in the morning! Can we look forward to an Arunachal Laughter Challenge?

HINDI: ARUNACHAL'S NEW MOTHER TONGUE

Of all the states of North East India, Arunachal is the only state without a distinct common language followed throughout the state. Assam has Assamese, Mizoram has Mizo, Manipur has Manipuri, Meghalaya has Khasi and Jaintia, Nagaland has Nagamese, Tripura has Bengali. In states like Nagaland, Mizoram and Meghalaya, English is spoken commonly.

Arunachal Pradesh has 28 major tribes, 100 sub tribes, 50 distinct languages and dialects. Unlike other six states, Hindi is the most commonly used language in Arunachal. Hindi movies and serials are commonly watched at homes and Hindi songs are very popular amongst all tribes. In fact TV shows like Arunachal Idol and Voice of Arunachal are dominated by Hindi songs. Hindi is the language of choice for proceedings in the Legislative assembly. Hindi is also the main language used for campaigning by all politicians and leaders.

This preponderance of Hindi as the language of choice is gradually leading to Hindi replacing native languages as the common language. Today most children prefer Hindi over native languages. In most schools, colleges, institutions and bazaars of Arunachal, Hindi is commonly spoken. Teachers teach in Hindi, Doctors converse with patients in Hindi, Commuters speak to autos/taxi driver in Hindi, Politicians give speeches in Hindi...! The increase in spoken Hindi has also led to names of persons changing over to Hindi names in preference to tribal names.

However, the Hindi spoken in Arunachal is much different from the Hindi spoken in mainland Hindi states like UP, Bihar, Delhi, MP etc in both grammar and pronunciation. Grammatically correct Hindi is rarely spoken and followed in Arunachal. In fact Hindi is spoken with a local accent and with many errors. Important Hindi traits like *Strilling* and *Pulling* are rarely followed in the Hindi spoken in the area. Pure Hindi scholars may not support our version of Hindi! In fact it is comical and funny to hear our politicians giving speeches in Hindi.

The predominance of Hindi may have also led to higher sense of patriotism and nationalism amongst most Arunachalese. With most national/patriotic songs in Sanskrit, Urdu or chaste Hindi, many Arunachalese understand and assimilate these songs better than other North Easterners.

The rise of Hindi has led to the decline of native languages in the region. Today a large number of our children speak mostly in Hindi; in fact many children do not speak native mother tongues at all. The rise of Hindi has also led to the decline of English language in the state. The quality of spoken and written English is declining at alarming trends. Hindi is important; but native languages and English are also equally important.

Most mainlanders may not believe that Mohammed Rafi, Kishore Kumar and Lata Mangeshkar are immensely popular in Arunachal Pradesh. In fact Arunachal Pradesh is by itself a fully Hindi name! However most natives pronounce it as ORUNASOL!

TYPICAL ARUNACHALI TOWN…!

It is interesting to visit any town of our great state. Most towns greet travellers with welcome gates. The initial shops after the welcome gates would be few tyre shops, mechanic/ welding/ fabrication units, *paan ghumties* and liquor shops. As we progress into the town the number of shops increase with the presence of banks, petrol pumps, hotels and hardware shops. The main bazaar would generally consist of grocery stores, cloth shops, stationary shops, few bakeries, small eating joints, hardware, electronic/ gift shops, hotels etc. There would be a daily market wherein local people would sell vegetables, fruits, small eateries, meat, fish etc.

Our towns are marked by motley of Bamboo/Wood/Straw houses and concrete buildings. The earlier Assam type houses with tin roofs are slowly giving way to RCC buildings extending to 3-4 floors. Since the bazaar areas are congested, the buildings have started extending vertically upwards. In the posh areas where the rich and powerful reside, tall concrete walls with barbed wire surround the compound. Huge metallic gates with cattle traps mark the entrance into the compound. These big residential compounds almost resemble central jails! Unlike houses on stilts generally seen in the villages, in towns most kutcha houses are constructed with floors at ground level. The wellness of people living in these kutcha houses is announced by the presence of swanky vehicles like Scorpio, Duster etc parked near the house.

On the dirtier side, generally there are garbage dumps at the entry of towns. There are a large number of *Paan Ghumties* selling all sorts of *Paan, Tamul, Supari, Paan Masala and Ghutka*. One of the most prominent litters would be the small plastic pouches or sachets of paan masala and ghutka. A keen observer may notice that there are more liquor shops and shops selling paan masala and ghutka than medicine shops! All liquor shops are protected with grills as if these were jewellery shops!! This means that effect of liquor and paan masala/ghutka is less on our people!! Our towns are also too dusty. For a pristine and crystal clear environment, there seems to be too much dust in our towns.

The appearance of these sleepy towns are deceptive in safety related issues. A few days rainfall exposes the planning/construction faults wherein major portions of the town are deluged with water. There are frequent fire accidents with losses amounting to crores of rupees. At some places there are no avenues for the few fire tenders to venture for fire fighting!! Maze of haphazard electric wires can be seen hanging from poles, buildings, transformers etc. It seems many people are tapping electricity directly from the wires.

There has been a recent boom in construction of rent houses at all major towns. The high demand for rent houses have been caused by the influx of large numbers of people from villages to the towns in search of better job prospects, better medical care and better education. It seems that almost everyone is constructing rent houses! Due to the influx of large numbers of people from villages to the towns and availability of easy money, land prices have sky rocketed. Land and real estate prices in major towns of Arunachal are at par if not higher than many mainland cities! Due to high demand of land, at towns located in hilly areas, one notices many hills being cut and dug up for creation of real estate. In the long term these rampant cutting of hills may lead to landslides, flooding and soil erosion.

Despite the boom in construction, our towns are still small, less populated and serene. Unplanned construction activity, cutting of forest areas/ hills for creation of real estate is spoiling the image/ appearance of our towns. There is a lot of scope for improvement in all aspects. One of the first steps maybe is to start planning the expansion of our towns. Creation of parks, playing areas, drainages etc may be followed up. All these may be implemented to convert our towns and villages into truly smart towns/villages!! Why wait for the government for the announcements and pronouncements for Smart Cities?

Towns and Cities Bursting at Seams

If any middle aged healthy man or woman tries to wear dresses they wore in their teenage years, most probably they would not fit into the dresses. Most probably they would have overgrown the teenage dresses and it's likely that the dress would bulge at many places!

Today, more and more people are migrating to urban towns and cities in search of better education for children, better facilities, better medical facilities and better lives! The increased migration is leading to increased houses, rent houses further leading to increase in colonies and settlements. New colonies and settlements are leading to increased shops, bazaars and offices. New areas with jungles, hills, rivulets are being developed for new settlements. The demand for new housing is such that many open areas, gardens, streams are also being encroached upon. In many cases even Govt areas and forest areas are not spared. These new settlements are mushrooming in an unplanned manner. Most expansions of the towns are dictated by local people with the local authorities reacting only after the colonies have come up!

Increased population in new settlements has multiplied the demand for new electric connections, water connections and infrastructure like roads, drainage etc. Due to unplanned expansion of our towns, the addition of new settlements is not being matched by similar increase in essential infrastructure like electricity, water supply, roads, drainages etc. This is leading to acute shortages of essential services like electricity, water supply, drainages, roads etc.

Increased population and increased income has also led to sharp increase in numbers of vehicles. There are so many vehicles that there is acute lack of parking space. One lane of many roads are just being used for parking vehicles only! Our roads are unable to cater to this increase in vehicles and traffic. Even in our small towns, there are chaotic traffic jams and commuters are spending hours in their vehicles. Sometimes it takes 2-3 hours to cover 15-20 km. The increase in vehicles has further led to increase in air pollution and temperatures are on the rise.

Due to contamination of drains and sewages with plastic packets and non degradable waste most drains and sewages are blocked. Due to lack of suitable drainage and blocked drains/sewerages, many roads, localities, bazaars get clogged with water accumulation after few hours of rainfall. Many of our roads are not constructed with any slope and few roads/localities do not have drains at all. This leads to water clogging and accumulation after few hours of rainfall.

To rectify these anomalies, municipal councils were recently established in many towns. However, with the enormity of the task at hand, in some cases the towns have become dirtier and chaotic after the formation of municipal councils! One solution maybe is to develop our small towns and villages into independent, clean and livable entities. May be that will slow down this craze of urban migration! We need to pay more attention to planning and expansion of our towns. Don't we want to live in clean, orderly and well planned towns? Shouldn't we be proud of our towns?

DECLINING FOREST COVER...!

As per Govt of India, Forest Survey of India Report 2013, amongst all the states of India, Arunachal Pradesh has the second largest forest cover in the country at 67,321 sq km of forest cover. In terms of percentage of forest cover with respect to total geographical area, Arunachal Pradesh is fourth highest with 80.39 percent.

However, as per the same reports, between 1989 to 2013 the forest covered area of Arunachal Pradesh has reduced by 1681 sq km. Between 2011 to 2013 the forest covered area of Arunachal Pradesh has reduced by 89 sq km.

Reduction in forest cover has been caused by variety of reasons including *Jhum* (shifting) cultivation, forest fires, legal and illegal timber business, conversion of forested areas for construction of houses/offices/irrigation fields, hill cutting to create real estate, firewood etc.

Old timers will vouch for the fact that areas around our villages/towns including the paths leading to them were covered by dense forests. Due to the dense forests, wild animals were occasionally spotted in these forests. Today the forests around our villages/towns and along the roads have been severely depleted. In most cases we may clearly see the other horizon or the foot hills through the sparse bushes!

Only those forests are surviving where humans/vehicles/elephants cannot venture due to rough terrain. At a small scale, some govt declared reserved forests are being preserved. Some trees/plants are being revived due to plantation crops like tea, rubber, orange, oil palm etc.

The recent phenomena of severe water shortage in drought hit states like Maharashtra, Karnataka, Telangana etc, the water clashes between states of Haryana, Punjab, Karnataka, Tamil Nadu etc, the abnormally high average temperatures in many places of mainland India should serve as a chilling reminder about the long term ill effects of deforestation.

It is still not too late to rectify these problems associated with deforestation.

One of the major sources of deforestation is widespread cutting of trees for firewood. The govt and social organisations should take a lead role in promoting the adaptation of biogas in our villages/towns for cooking/heating requirements. Govt may subsidize the installation of biogas plants. Access and availability of cooking gas may be expanded to our villages. Availability and usage of cooking gas is presently negligible in our villages. This will reduce the cutting of trees for firewood.

We all should voluntarily avoid using wood in the construction of our houses/buildings. Wood may be replaced with cheaper and easily available alternatives like wood composites, plastic wood, plastic etc. Use of bamboo in house construction may also be encouraged.

Illegal timber business by using bench saws or hand saws in certain areas should be banned and strictly implemented.

The govt and social organisations should also take a lead role in planting more trees. This may be promoted through horticulture or other plantation crops like tea, rubber, oil palm, orange etc.

The govt and other organisations may also consider networking all offices to achieve a paperless office. Paperless offices are in practice in many places. This will lead to a huge reduction in usage of paper (wood product) in our offices.

As responsible citizens, our aim should be to leave behind a Healthy Earth/Environment for next generation Arunachalese who can taste fresh air and fresh water.

CREATING MORE JOBS...!

As per Arunachal Pradesh Annual Planning document of 2011-12, Arunachal Pradesh continues to remain poorest of the poor State with inadequate basic infrastructure and low economic growth. The unemployment figures for Arunachal are also the second highest in the country!

Unemployment is one of the major reasons for unwanted activities like theft, crime, extortion, insurgency etc. Unemployment is also one of the main reasons for drugs/alcohol addiction.

Government jobs/vacancies are gradually being saturated. Lesser and lesser jobs will be offered by the government. Recently the doctor's retirement age has been increased from 58 yrs to 62 years. The retirement age of other government employees has been increased from 58 to 60 years. This will lead to lesser job vacancies being created by the government. With increasing numbers of educated youth, job demands are multiplying. There are many unemployed youth in the state.

How do we increase job opportunities in the state?

One of the quickest ways to provide employment is by setting up more industries in the state. New industries will result in creation of large number of jobs. In addition, other benefits will be accrued in terms of supporting infrastructure/ jobs like transportation, hotel, restaurants, banking etc in addition to more revenues for the state!

There are negligible industries in the state. The single most negative factor against setting up of industries in the state is the lack of stabilised three phase electric supply in the industrial estates! No industry can sustain without stabilised three phase electricity supply. It appears that this simple aspect has not been paid adequate attention by our planners.

The other major problem is the lack of Single Window Clearance for setting up industries. Presently, Industry Licence is from a different *Window*, Trading Licence is from a different *Window*, Municipal/ Pollution Clearances are from different *Windows*, VAT/ CST registrations are from different *Windows*....etc. Creation of a truly Single Window Clearance will lead to faster establishment and operationalisation of new industries.

The second major avenue at job creation is the development of tourism in the state. With many pristine and exotic locations, Arunachal Pradesh has the potential to be a major tourist destination. Increase in tourism will lead to increase in supporting infrastructure/ jobs like transportation, hotel, restaurants, shops etc. However, for tourism to develop the govt has to build all weather roads and provide electricity in these exotic tourist locations. Presently the roads to most tourist destinations are in bad condition.

Another major job creation opportunity is the establishment of Central Institutes and major projects in the state. Central institutes including educational institutes will lead to job creation for native people. Similarly, major projects like Hydro Power Projects, Railways, Airports etc will create more jobs for natives.

There is a lot of work being done towards improving infrastructure in the state. However a lot more needs to be done towards establishment of more industries and improving tourism in the state.

Don't we all want our children and relatives to be gainfully employed? Don't we want to see our native brothers and sisters lead decent lives? Don't we want to see a developed Arunachal Pradesh?

Serving outside the State

Many Arunachalese hesitate to serve outside the state. After completion of professional degrees like Engineering, Medical, Law etc most Arunachalese want to come back and serve within the state. Many Arunachalese hesitate to serve outside the state as they get homesick very easily. Arunachalese miss their rustic, simple villages nestled in lush green forests, miss Arunachali dishes, miss the fresh air/water and desire to come back at the earliest. The hesitancy to serve outside the state is such an extent that there are unemployed associations in the State!

However, there is already a saturation of jobs in the state govt. The recent decision of the state govt to increase retirement age of doctors from 58 to 62 years and other employees from 58 to 60 years will block job openings for the youth. The only way to create more jobs is through creation of more industries and services sector like tourism, hospitality etc. But with very poor infrastructure like dilapidated roads, very poor electricity supply, lack of airports and railways, new job openings in industries and tourism is some time away. As per latest figures, the unemployment figures for Arunachal is among the highest in the nation.

There are thousands of job openings in all India services like IAS, IPS, Allied services, Railways, Public Sector Undertakings like ONGC, IOC, SAIL, GAIL, BSNL, NHPC etc. There are many more challenging careers like the Indian Armed forces comprising of the Army, Navy, Air Force and Para Military forces like CRPF, BSF, ITBP, CISF, SSB etc. There are jobs for engineers, doctors, law graduates and graduates/post graduates for both men and women.

There are many job openings at the world level also. There are job openings in the United Nations organisations like WHO, UNICEF, UNESCO etc. There are job openings in organisations like Merchant Navy, Shipping

Corporations, Civil Aviation organisations etc which would allow men and women to serve and travel in various corners of the world. Today very few Arunachalese are working in remote countries of the world.

Our youth need to compete with other mainland candidates and grab jobs in these central services. Employment in central services will allow our youth to see more places, interact with more people from different races, cultures etc. This will broaden our horizons and our customs and traditions would be spread across the country and world. We can learn from other races and tribes and carry back these better ideas back to our nation and state.

If we keep competing within ourselves within our state we will not improve much and enrich our knowledge due to limited scope in the state. We need to compete with mainland Indians and foreigners in different fields to keep improving ourselves and to remain abreast with higher standards of skills, education and research.

Wouldn't it better to have Arunachalese employed gainfully outside the state in challenging jobs compared to having unemployed associations in the state? Are you willing to serve outside the state?

EXPENSIVE LIVING IN ARUNACHAL...!

Arunachalese will agree that almost everything is more expensive in our state compared to neighbouring Assam and other states. The cost of most items is higher by 10-15 %. It certain items, the price difference is almost 50-200 %!

Prices of grocery items like rice, dal, atta etc are almost 10-15 % higher than Assam. Fruits and vegetables are costlier by 15-40 %. Eggs, Poultry, Fish and meat are also costlier in our state by 15-30 %. One example is mangoes costing 70-80 per kg at Margherita, Jonai or Harmuti costs 100-120 in Arunachal!

Construction items like cement, rods, tin sheets, kitchen items etc are also costlier. Electrical items are also costlier. For major construction work, almost all items are procured from Assam.

Due to the high costs of items in Arunachal Pradesh, many people are resorting to buying items from Assam. It may be seen that many Arunachalese visit the supporting Assam towns like Harmuti, Lakhimpur, Silapathar, Jonai, Balipara, Tinsukia, Naharkatiya, Margherita etc during Sundays/ market days.

The only few items cheaper in Arunachal maybe are wood, petrol/diesel and liquor!

Therefore it may be safely concluded that the average cost of living is more in Arunachal by 10-15 %.

Items are costlier in Arunachal due to many factors. The foremost cause for costlier items is transportation cost to this remote corner. The other cause is because we are importing majority of items, with negligible manufacturing/production in the state. Even eggs, fish, poultry, fruits and vegetables are imported from outside.

The other cause maybe is whimsical pricing of items. Retailers routinely charge above MRP quoting less availability and high pricing by distributors. Many people quote higher taxes in Arunachal for the higher prices of most items.

If the economy of the state is poor and average Arunachalese are poorer, then it is logical to have lesser taxes so that prices of items in the state is comparative if not cheaper than Assam. It also follows that if prices of items are comparative, most people will buy items from shops/dealers in Arunachal.

As a result, majority of Arunachal money is being channelized into Assam/other states. Every time Arunachalese buy items from Assam and other states, it helps the economy of those states. You are aware of booming townships of Tinsukia, Margherita, Naharkatia, Dibrugarh, Jonai, Silapathar, Lakhimpur, Harmuti, Tezpur booming and expanding on Arunachali money!

In order to ensure circulation of Arunachalese money within the state, one way is to re-analyse and revamp the tax regime of the state to make prices comparable with Assam. The other way is to promote and push products of Arunachal Pradesh. For example, there may be a rule for traders to compulsorily procure at least 30-50 % of their sold items from local sources. Most products sold in the state are procured from outside the state. This move will help the local entrepreneurs, farmers and economy.

The state leadership needs to study this aspect of higher price of items in Arunachal and initiate necessary steps for reducing the flow of Arunachalese money to neighbouring states. After all it is our hard earned money!

Infrastructural Collapse during Natural Calamities

Recent rains and weather phenomena has exposed the poor quality and poor planning of various infrastructure like roads, bridges, electricity etc. From western areas of Tawang, Bomdila and Seppa to the southern areas of Tirap, Changlang and Namsai, there were floods, landslides, mudslides leading to road blockages. Many roads to remote areas were cut off resulting in marooned citizens, ration shortages in remote towns and villages. In some cases mudslides and floods led to loss of precious lives and property.

Towards construction of highways in the state, earth cutting and adequate protection have not been planned and executed with foresight. This has led to loosening of the hill sides leading to landslides and mud slides. In addition to causing road blockages, these landslides and mudslides have resulted in many lives being lost along with loss of homes and property. Many common Arunachalese have also contributed to mudslides and landslides by rampant earth cutting for creating infrastructure without proper studies and analysis.

Most of our infrastructures like roads, electric lines/towers, mobile towers, bridges etc break down even in mild weather phenomena like rains, windy conditions, local storms etc. Breaking down of essential infrastructure in mild weather indicates poor quality materials and workmanship. During emergency situations like natural calamities these vital infrastructure like roads, railways, bridges, hospitals, airports, electricity and mobile towers would be required for rescue and relief operations. Availability of these critical infrastructures will save many lives during and after natural calamities. Therefore these critical infrastructures needs to be treated as the last line of defence and needs to be planned and constructed well.

Poor quality of infrastructure results from acceptance of sub standard work due to leakages of funds and due to *Chalta Hai* attitude. Natural calamities occur all over India and in other parts of the world. But critical infrastructure does not fail easily and even if they fail, they are repaired in quick time. Quick recovery and repairs of critical infrastructures ensure that normal life resumes at the earliest.

During the recent rains, many of our major towns including Itanagar were cut off and troubled by roads and bridges getting washed away and electric towers/lines breaking down or collapsing at many places. Many towns like Pasighat and Aalo were without electricity and poor mobile connectivity for many days. Even the newly constructed 132 KVA tower line inaugurated by the Chief Minister himself collapsed! We need to learn from these incidents and construct alternate roads to connect our towns. We also need to carry out an audit of all vulnerable areas and find lasting solutions. We need to be prepared since Arunachal & North East are located in the severest Seismic Zone 5!

True test of quality is when infrastructures like roads, bridges, towers, electricity stand up during bad weather conditions. Has poor quality become a part and parcel of our lives? Are common citizens supposed to suffer silently without complaining! What might happen if an actual cyclone hits us?

TAX & OFFICE TAX....!

Common citizens pay tax to the Govt for buying every commodity and goods from the market...citizens pay tax for buying Petrol/Diesel...citizens pay Road Tax...citizens pay fees for licences (Trading/Industry/driving licences)... citizens pay the Govt for goods and services (GST/ VAT etc)...citizens pay the Govt for vehicles (Registration, Plying Licence, Fitness/ Pollution certificates etc)...citizens pay for Stamp papers. Every time citizens register an affidavit/ lease deed/sale deed they pay the govt.

Citizens pay the Govt for electricity, water, municipal services. Citizens pay the Govt for eating in a restaurant, going to a beauty parlour, watching a movie, flying in a plane, travelling in railways. Common men pay for visiting a zoo, visiting a historical centre or a museum. Every time we use credit/ debit card we pay the govt. There are toll plazas collecting taxes for using various roads and bridges. In fact citizens are taxed before birth and even after death!

Even for constructing houses, in addition to paying for cement, rods, tin sheets etc citizens have to pay for *Gitti/Ballu, Stones* etc to the govt and to quarry owners. Today we have to pay for picnic spots also! The only thing available free for all is probably only 'Air'!

To add to all these, citizens have to pay for many types of routine forms issued by Govt offices like Treasury Challan, Pollution forms, Trading licence forms, Application forms, Inner Line permits etc. Citizens have to pay for ST/PRC forms, school admission forms etc. Patients pay even for OPD Registration in General Hospitals. In fact many officials are charging money for putting office seals. The officer signs inside the office and stamps/seals are put outside the office by staff with charges varying from Rs 100 to 200/- per stamp/seal. Regarding medical fitness certificate for driving licence/

students, the signature of the doctor maybe free but we have to pay for the stamp/seal at the office!

The other recent phenomenon is 'Processing Fees' charged in many offices. For most of these 'almost legalised' fees no receipts are provided. These 'Legal Fees' are taken by many officials with a straight face and without any guilt or remorse! It is surprising that common citizens pay these 'Legal Fees' without opposition. To add to these are the unaccounted charges at various Check gates and *Nakas*. All check gates manned by police or departments charge various amounts for services and to just pass through the gates!

It is estimated this disruptive parallel economy is worth hundreds of crores! With this money collected from villagers and innocent public, the govt can finance infrastructure projects like roads, water supply system or school education/healthcare can be made free!

Should common citizens pay for routine forms like ST/PRC/OPD Registration etc? Should common citizens be charged for seals, stamps and signatures? One simple solution maybe is to fill up all these routine forms online!

Like they say "There are no Free Lunches...!". The only silver lining seems to be the fact that at least Arunachalese presently do not pay Income Tax!

TOO MUCH POLITICS

With the conduct of general elections in India and simultaneous elections in Arunachal Pradesh, the political scenario is on high heat with political gamesmanship, political manoeuvring, accusations & counter-allegations dominating all electronic, print & social media. Almost every electronic, print & social media are dominated by political news only. Shouting matches, heated arguments by spokespersons & representatives of different political parties dominate TV shows. Majority press releases are about complaints and wrong doings of other parties.

It is also seen that most of our villages and towns are dominated by political discussions and gossips. One can spot many groups in remote villages discussing politics. Even children and youth are politically aware and talk about Modi, Rahul, Pema, Mamata, Conrad etc! Most conversations end up with "So...Who is winning the elections?" Thereafter most villagers, common citizens turn into expert psephologists or election experts! In fact it appears that many villages are totally divided by political affiliations. It seems there is too much politics in our lives!

Aristotle quoted in 350 BC that "man is by nature a political animal." Politics is an essential part of any democracy. There is political manoeuvring in Autocracies, Communism, Socialism and Kingdoms also. In fact there is politics in social organisations, village societies, NGOs and even in our families. It is known that there are political considerations for appointment of key senior personnel in any govt.

However, when politics starts overshadowing everything else, merit and capabilities take a back seat and society starts deteriorating and decaying. Once elections are over and governments are formed, politicians should transform into leaders and good administrators focussing on development, progress, peace & stability in society. Politicians should appoint capable and progressive persons to key senior posts to ensure fair and efficient administration. If required professionals and experts from private institutions or public may also be drafted into the administration via lateral entry system.

It seems that everyone is an expert in politics. The expertise in politics is not corroborating with good governance and administration. Recent results of board examinations show dismal performance in Class XII & Class X exams. Newly constructed roads & highways are deteriorating, power lines are malfunctioning, buildings/bridges are collapsing and infrastructure failing!

Question to ask is does any Govt have major impact on the lives of common citizens that their lives are transformed for the better? Does a new govt lead to eradication of poverty, corruption, efficient governance and a fair administration? Does a new govt change our lives majorly?

If there are no major changes to the lifestyle & livelihood of common citizens, then why so much fuss about elections and politics. We should carry on doing our duties and responsibilities diligently and pay less attention to politics. Point to ponder; can we live life peacefully and progress without politics? If yes let's talk, discuss and involve in Less Politics! Do you agree?

CLEAN ELECTIONS

The ongoing simultaneous elections in 'peace loving' Arunachal Pradesh have been fiercely contested amidst reports of violent incidents, arson, assault on govt officials, use of money & muscle power. Bridges have been intentionally dismantled, helipads have been booby trapped by bombs to ensure that re-polling benefits certain candidates!

As per reports, more than Rupees 6 Crores cash has been seized along with liquor worth more than 2 Crores! As per election watchdog Association for Democratic Reforms as many as 29 (16 %) of total 184 candidates contesting the Assembly elections have criminal cases against them. As per the same report, 131 (71 %) candidates are 'crorepatis' with the average assets being Rs 9.86 crore.

As per many reports, most candidates along with parties have spent about 10-20 crores or more during the elections. It is reported that votes are simply being sold to the highest bidder. These types of elections based on money power, muscle power and clan politics needs to be discouraged and curtailed during future elections.

A model of 'clean election' is being followed successfully in Mizoram. Organisatons like Mizo People's Forum (MPF) and supported by the Church plays the role of a watchdog. It issues guidelines on dos and don'ts and insists on low-key campaigns and the political parties adhere to them. Local unit members of the MPF must accompany a candidate during campaigning to check possible offers of cash and other allurements, and party workers are not allowed to campaign on behalf of a candidate. Compared to polls elsewhere, the Mizoram elections passed off peacefully without a single incident of violence or disturbance.

Similarly, in our state also, the Apatani Youth Association has made candidates sign a Memorandum of Understanding (MoU) with a promise not to use money or muscle power for votes during the campaign. The MoU strictly stipulates that candidates should not bribe voters with money or any other materials and should not indulge in any activity that may cause hatred or tension. It also prohibits using caste, community or religion for securing votes, not to set up camps in villages, not to campaign beyond 9 pm, not to indulge in booth capturing etc. A similar model may be implemented during next elections. A Pan-Arunachal, Inter-Tribe Clean Elections Monitoring & Implementation Committee should be formed and measures for clean elections strictly enforced else the candidates would be disqualified! The main points should include ban on use of money & muscle power, ban on clan/religion politics, ban on use of liquor, ban on door-to-door campaigning etc. Candidates should be allowed to address voters in Community Halls, selected rallies, through manifesto, TV/Radio etc.

This type of gross misuse of money & muscle power should be discouraged at all levels. If the candidates use these humongous amounts to win elections, they would be busy recovering the amount and amassing money for the next elections, diverting money meant for development! The huge amount of money saved by clean politics will benefit politicians, public and Arunachal Pradesh.

ELECTIONOMICS: PUBLIC MONEY BACK TO PUBLIC!

Post elections, the markets of towns and villages of Arunachal Pradesh are buzzing with activity. It is almost as if a new festival bigger than our traditional festivals has swept Arunachal! Suddenly the buying power of common citizens has gone up. One can spot villagers buying large numbers of clothes, blankets, utensils, chairs, cookers, refrigerators, washing machines etc. One can spot many Pick Up Trucks filled with these newly bought items being transported back to the villages. In fact a dealer commented that he has run out of refrigerators, washing machines and TVs!

During Election season there has been multi-fold jump in the business of Petrol pumps, Liquor shops, Grocery shops, Digital Printers, Audio/Video studios and Vehicle dealers. Petrol Pumps witnessed unending lines of two-wheelers and vehicles filling up tanks with 'Coupons' from different candidates. Though 'Dry Days' and early closures were enforced by social organisations/ administration, thousands of cases of IMFL and beer were procured by different candidates. The grocery stores saw huge sales of Rice, Dal, Potatoes, oil etc due candidates feeding thousands of volunteers and supporters every day during the election period. In fact there was no pork available in the market of many towns! Digital Printers remained busy printing thousands of pamphlets, posters, flex banners. Banks also witnessed jump in cash flow and banking activity. One banker commented that few bank branches ran out of liquid cash during election season due large withdrawal by candidates and parties!

The towns are witnessing traffic jams due to increase in vehicles during election season. Candidates from Arunachal hired all available vehicles from nearby Assam for campaigning. In fact many key supporters and mobilisers were rewarded with new Scorpios, Boleros, Tractors etc. There is a sudden increase in the numbers of Royal Enfield Bullets and Scooties supplied by candidates! Many vehicle dealers are seeing multi-fold jump in vehicle sales!

As per many election analysts and reports, many common voters in Arunachal have earned large amounts of money & material amounting to about 40,000-50,000 during election season. In constituencies with lesser voters, voters are reported to have earned even more!

The analyst also commented that there would be indirect spin offs as a result of this money flow. There would be shortage of local labourers for at least another month and work would suffer. Since these huge amounts of money have been spent, winning candidates will recover the spent amount; as a result developmental projects in the State would suffer or slow down.

Another election expert had the parting words. These huge amounts were public money in the first place. This is an oxymoronese justice that Public Money has Gone Back to the Public! Point to ponder-Is this election story a Tragedy or a Comedy?

LOTTERIES, HOUSIES & CALENDARS

The recent phenomena gripping our state are the preponderance of Lotteries, Housies and Calendars! Many festivals, clan celebrations/ gatherings, institution anniversary celebrations are resorting to Lotteries, Housies and Calendars to generate funds.

There are so many clans...Father's Clan...Mother's Clan...Wife's Father's Clan...Wife's Mother's Clan...Own Tribe...Wife's Tribe...Own Town...Own Colony...Alumni Association etc. Then there are festivals and Mega Festivals. Each of these events is marked by celebrations of various types spread over few days. These celebrations include community feasts, cultural programmes, games and sports etc. Many of these events include Celebrity Nights and Fashion shows. The celebrity nights include invitation to Bollywood Stars and famous singers/comedians. Many of these Bollywood stars demand fees in tens of lakhs excluding travel and accommodation expenses for their support teams consisting of many members. In fact any festival or celebration is not worth it if there are no celebrities or fashion shows!

With this kind of expenditures running into lakhs and crores of rupees, resource mobilisation is a critical factor for the success of any major festival or celebration. In many festivals or celebrations, most funds are generated from Govt sources. However a major portion of funds are required to be generated by resource mobilisation teams. The easiest way to generate funds is through conduct of Lotteries and Housies. Lottery tickets costing anywhere from Rs 200 to Rs 2000 per ticket. Housie tickets vary from Rs 500 to Rs 10,000/-. With these kinds of ticket prices, the top prizes vary from new JCBs, Scorpio vehicles, new Duster vehicles, Royal Enfield Bullet motorcycles etc. In fact there are some lotteries offering prize money in crores; and there are many buyers also! Of course more than half of the generated money is retained in the corpus funds to conduct these festivals or celebrations!

These Lotteries, Housies have become a burden on Govt employees, most middle and upper income groups. Many citizens are given the responsibilities to sell off entire lottery books going into many thousands. It is estimated that many households are dealing with Lotteries and Housies worth lakhs of rupees annually. This is despite the fact that there is an existing Govt order banning gambling in all forms and Housies!

A rough estimate reveals expenditures of multiple crores on festivals and celebrations only. If Govt and communities use these huge funds for developmental activities our communities and state would have progressed a bit. We have huge funds for festivals, celebrations, clan festivals... however we have less funds for social projects, infrastructure, industrial projects, education, healthcare etc and our state has one of the highest unemployment rates in the country!

Should we carry on donating huge amounts to so many festivals, celebrations and clan festivals?

Bandh Days!

Bandhs are routinely called in India; especially the North East region. There are Bharat bandhs, state bandhs, district bandhs, area bandhs, tribe/caste bandhs, economic bandhs, transporters bandh etc. In fact many bandhs are enforced by small groups of people with police and administration becoming mute spectators. Bandh calls are so common in North East that many people cater for bandhs while planning for major festivals or events! Most citizens are now accustomed to postponing travel plans or travelling late in the night to beat bandh timings. There have been many incidents of violence by bandh organisers against commuters and common people.

However, bandh days are unusual quiet days also. For people living in towns and cities, it is a pleasure to wake up to soundless days. We get so used to hearing all sorts of noises made by so many vehicles, two wheelers, generators that we do not realise the bliss of silence! Even electric supply is steady since many major electric consumers like shops, offices, garages and factories are closed. There are health benefits also during bandh days. With vehicles off the roads, one gets to breathe fresh, unpolluted air giving our lungs a much needed respite from contaminated/polluted air. If one has to visit any relative or hospital during bandh days, the only option is walking!

During bandh days, schools/colleges are closed, offices are closed, shops and bazaars are closed, factories are closed and everyone stays at home. Students and office goers enjoy bandhs since they don't have to go to school or office. So bandh days provide opportunities for spending quality time with our family members. One can complete pending household work and catch up on hobbies. Increased family time allows bonding with family members thus helping in healthy relationships within family members.

However, some citizens do suffer during these bandhs. Casual labourers cannot earn their daily wages, daily wage earners have to make it up the next day. Some citizens have to re-schedule or cancel their travel plans. There may be some harassment to patients travelling for medical treatment and students travelling to their school/colleges. There are occasions when commuters travel late in the night to reach destinations outside the Bandh timings. Office work and business plans have to be postponed for a day. There are no business transactions or factory production during bandhs.

However, there is an additional benefit accrued during recent bandh days. With the ongoing FIFA World Cup in football, it is a bonus during bandh days as fans can watch their late night football matches without bothering about waking late next morning!

Bandhs are commonly held to oppose injustice, price rise, lack of civic amenities, unresolved criminal cases, interstate / inter tribe conflicts, politics etc. However, any clues as to why there are no bandhs organised against corruption?

Unemployment & Job Creation...!

There is an emerging crisis in Arunachal Pradesh and North East; growing unemployment amongst the restive youth of the region. As per State's Annual Planning document of 2011-12, Arunachal continues to remain poorest of the poor State with inadequate basic infrastructure and low economic growth. The unemployment figures for Arunachal are also the second highest in the country! As per state's labour department's data, about 67,000 youths were registered as unemployed in 2018.

Unemployment is one of the major reasons for unwanted activities like theft, crime, extortion, insurgency etc. Unemployment is also one of the main reasons for drugs/alcohol addiction. Many experts relate the recent anti-PRC rioting and arson in the Capital Complex to growing unemployment.

Government jobs/vacancies are gradually being saturated. Lesser and lesser jobs will be offered by the government. With increasing numbers of educated youth, job demands are multiplying.

One of the quickest ways to provide employment is by setting up more industries in the state. New industries will result in creation of large number of jobs. In addition, other benefits will be accrued in terms of supporting infrastructure/ jobs like transportation, hotel, restaurants, banking etc.

There are negligible industries in the state. The major negative factors against setting up of industries in the state is the lack of stabilised three phase electric supply in the industrial estates, lack of supporting ecosystem, lack of transportation network etc. No industry can sustain without stabilised three phase electricity supply.

The other major problem is the lack of Single Window Clearance for setting up industries. Presently, Industry Licence is from a different *Window*, Trading Licence is from a different *Window*, Municipal/ Pollution Clearances are from different *Windows*, VAT/ CST/GST registrations are from different *Windows*...etc. Creation of a truly Single Window Clearance will lead to faster establishment and operationalisation of new industries.

The second major avenue at job creation is the development of tourism in the state. With many pristine and exotic locations, Arunachal Pradesh has the potential to be a major tourist destination. Increase in tourism will lead to increase in supporting infrastructure/ jobs like transportation, hotel, restaurants, shops etc. However, for tourism to develop the govt has to build all weather roads and provide electricity in these exotic tourist locations. Presently the roads to most tourist destinations are in bad condition.

There is a lot of work being done towards improving infrastructure in the state. However a lot more needs to be done towards establishment of more industries and improving tourism in the state.

Once industries are created, the state must support these local industries with strict implementation of Preferential Buying and Preferential Pricing. All govt departments and state organisations must compulsorily procure products from local industries only.

Don't we all want our children and relatives to be gainfully employed? Don't we want to see our native brothers and sisters lead decent lives? Don't we want to see a developed Arunachal Pradesh?

INVASION OF TECHNOLOGY

Rapid advances in technology have a major impact on our lives. New appliances, new applications and new technologies have altered the way we work, the way we live and the way we enjoy! Newer technology has transformed our slower, lazier lifestyle to faster, busier, well connected lifestyle. Today, most things work at the click of a button or touch of a finger tip!

Many appliances considered indispensible previously have been rendered redundant by newer technology. The many household items made redundant by technology include VCR/VCD Players, Cassette players, Landline phones, FAX Machines, Cable TV Etc. Electronic photography has led to the redundancy of Photo Studios, Photo Albums. Today all photos and videos are electronically stored in computers and hard drives.

Formerly many people relied on kerosene operated lanterns for light, kerosene operated stoves for cooking. Just a few years ago, towns and villages were dotted with STD Booths used by people to call and talk to friends and relatives. Today there are no STD booths; rather use of landline telephones is gradually becoming redundant. Earlier one could spot numerous bullock carts, horse carts used to transport men and material. Earlier one could spot many buffaloes and bullocks required for ploughing the fields. The advent of tractors and 4 wheel drive vehicles have lessened the requirements of buffaloes and bullocks for ploughing or for carrying men and material.

Previously erudite people used to go to libraries to study books and to refer to encyclopaedias and reference books. Today libraries are rarely used and encyclopaedias are rarely referred to. People are not even referring to dictionaries. Everything is searched on Google, Yahoo on mobiles and lap tops. Classic books are giving way to e books and Kindle versions.

Smart Mobile Phones single headedly turned many older appliances redundant. The facilities embedded in the single Smart Phone led to the redundancies of Cameras, Handy cams, Torch lights, Calculators, Alarm Clocks and Calendars! Smart phone applications like what's app, Xender, SMS, Scanner etc has made FAX Machines, Scanners totally redundant. Smart phones have emerged as the most valuable multipurpose gadget for one and all.

The way technology is leap frogging ahead, soon many present day appliances are facing redundancy threats. These include Desk Top Computers, Incandescent Light Bulbs, SMS/MMS, Calculators, Books, Paper money, wallets, wrist watches etc. With the impending advent of electric vehicles, soon petrol pumps may also become redundant!

Newer technologies are affecting human character and behaviour also. Modern gadgets are making humans lazier, inactive, unhealthy, manner less and individualistic. However, certain seamless and timeless human values like Integrity, Honesty, Strong Character etc should be strong enough to withstand the onslaught by the vices of new technologies. If humans lose these core values also, the future of human life would be in peril. The survival of human race would depend on preservation of these core values irrespective of new technologies. Can we sustain these core values?

Our World in 2050 AD

How would be the world be 30 years hence in 2050 AD? The world is transforming rapidly driven by technological advances which are inducing behavioural changes. Many appliances, technologies, thought process in vogue today will undergo rapid changeovers. Many important technologies are rendered redundant and become extinct within few decades only. The only constant is change!

Fax machines, type writers, cassette players, VCRs, cameras, alarm clocks, STD Booths are examples of appliances which have been rendered redundant in the last few years. Similarly ink pens, razor blades, photo albums, radio, telegram, CDs, Incandescent light bulbs, walkman, calculators, landline phones, cable TV etc are on the verge of disappearing!

With these rapid changes, what would be the world be in 2050? Some predictable change would be the advent of Electric vehicles. Electric vehicles will lead to reduction of diesel/petrol vehicles which in turn would lead to the vanishing of petrol pumps in the next few years. This would be followed by the introduction of automatic, driverless vehicles. Driverless vehicles would lead to non-requirement of drivers for vehicles!

The world will also see increased use of Solar and Wind energy leading to less usage of fossil fuels for electricity requirements. Entire houses, shops, resorts, offices would run on standalone solar energy totally off the grid.

Travelling would become much faster with bullet trains and hyperloops. Airliners will fly at hypersonic speeds (Multiple times speed of sound) which would allow commuters to cut down travel times in multiples. Commuters would be able to fly Guwahati to Delhi in half hour! Like cars and bikes most families & individuals will own pilotless aeroplanes. There would be aeroplanes parked in garages of houses!

Other technologies/appliances that are likely to become redundant include Ink Signatures, Keys, Charging Cables, Paper money, Debit & Credit Cards etc.

Rapid global warming will lead to rising sea levels and many low lying cities/ countries like Maldives, Bangladesh, Mumbai may disappear under water.

There would be several advances in medicines for treatment of dreaded diseases like Cancer. Stem cell and nanotechnology research may lead to delaying of aging, cure of many diseases. Life expectancy is likely to go up and there would be many persons above 90 & 100 years age. However there may be emergence of new diseases, more antibiotic resistant diseases or Re-emergence of Infectious Diseases like corona virus.

30 years hence in Arunachal there would be overall development in roads, railways, airports. All district HQs and major towns would be well connected. There would be uninterrupted electricity supply without voltage fluctuations to all villages and towns. Arunachal would emerge as major hotspot for tourists world over. Many industries would emerge in the state leading to almost all products being manufactured in the state. 30 years hence, Inner Line may be abolished and Income Tax would be paid by Arunachalese! Are you ready for the new world?

Pristine & Salubrious Winters

Winters in North East, especially in Arunachal Pradesh are a delight to experience. The weather is cool & salubrious, air is crystal clear, you can see hundreds of kilometres up to the snow clad mountains and the general mood is festive and buoyant. During clear winter nights, one can spot millions of stars sparkling in the clear sky along with Milky Way and other Galaxies. I

The landscape of valleys and meadows are a treat to the eyes, the numerous rivers & streams are crystal clear and the light breeze are all enriching to the eyes, heart and souls. This pristine environment attracts thousands of tourists making a beeline for these spots to see and experience themselves. With the opening up of Sadiya, Bomjir, Bogibeel, Sisirri bridges and improvements in roads & railways, tourists from neighbouring states and even from other countries have jumped multi-fold.

The salubrious weather and pristine environment attracts large numbers of avid picnickers. Many picnics are organised by various families, clans, organisations, classmates groups etc. Plentiful picnic parties from neighbouring states also can be spotted. Along the countryside, picnic parties can be spotted at most available stream, river or valleys. Along most roads one can spot picnic parties in hired buses and other vehicles buzzing ahead with blaring music of all kinds.

A few places experience snowfall in winters. Many tourist from neighbouring states rush to these places to see and experience snow in the mountains and valleys. Many people in the neighbouring states have never seen snowfall! Places like Tawang, Mechuka and Mayudia are attracting thousands of tourists causing traffic jams!

Most important family/clan events like clan get-togethers, marriages, death anniversaries are organised during winter. The crystal clear waters also see the increase in tourism activities like adventure sports, river rafting, trekking etc.

Winter also sees the availability of green leafy vegetables, fresh and delicious fruits like Apple, Oranges, Kiwis, Valencia, and Persimmon. Many flowers like dahlia, roses, petunia, marigold also bloom turning the landscape more beautiful. Enthusiasts can also spot large number of migratory birds from as far as Russia and Europe.

Winter is a season for festivals, parties, re-unions, picnics and vacations. One can hear singing, dancing and laughter all around. Many festivals also occur during winter. Winter is the time to get cozy under blankets and warm clothes. Unlike summers, during winter, one can spot many people sitting out soaking in the warmth of the Sun.

However winter is also associated with lethargy and inactivity. People stop going out, stop exercising and general activity reduces. Due to this inactivity, humans become more vulnerable to diseases during winter.

However, this winter season is a precursor to something more warming. The reason is the upcoming elections scheduled to be held soon. Arunachal is special because both parliamentary and assembly elections are planned to be held simultaneously. With political activities heating up, Arunachalese can feel some warmth!!

DAR KE AAGE JEET HAIN..!

What is common between Tapi Mra, Tine Mena, Anshu Jamsenpa and Taka Tamut? They are all Arunachalese who successfully climbed Mt Everest, the highest peak of the world. There is another aspect common to all of them; all of them overcame fear to successfully summit Mt Everest!

Similar is the story of Astronauts, Fighter Pilots, Submariners, Commandoes, Sky Divers and Parachute Jumpers. All of them experience fear; fear of height, fear of injury, fear of drowning, fear of the unknown, fear of death etc. In all these cases fear is overcome incrementally with training, exposure and experience. All these persons learn to overcome fear with perseverance, grit and sheer determination to excel in their respective fields.

Most successful candidates of competitive exams like UPSC, APPSC, IIT, IIM, AIIMS etc overcome fear of failure, fear of ridicule by following a strenuous study/tuition routine. Likewise successful Writers, Artists and Singers overcome fear of failure, fear of ridicule by perseverance, hard work and persistence. JK Rowling, the famous writer and author of the Harry Potter series is a great example. Her written works were rejected dozens of times by many publishers before becoming the best seller in the history of fiction!

Similarly many entrepreneurs and industrialists take great risks with big investments. Entrepreneurs and Industrialists introduce new products, new ideas in the market with a fear of rejection by the public leading to failure of the project. They overcome fear of failure in business, fear of bankruptcy, fear of ridicule by detailed preparation, hard work and innovation to emerge successful.

There's a fitting quote *"If you want to conquer fear, don't sit at home and think about it. Go out and do it"*. To be achievers, one has to step out of the comfort zones and challenge oneself. After we conceive a new project or plan, unless we take the first step towards achieving the selected goal and keep taking step after step, we cannot realise our dreams. A group of persons saw a dream that humans can land on the Moon. The group planned in detail, executed their plan and successfully landed on the moon-not once but many times! Today humans are planning to land on planet Mars!!

Many successful persons in the world like Mahatma Gandhi, Abraham Lincoln, Nelson Mandela, APJ Abdul Kalam, astronaut Yuri Gagarin, Tenzing Norgay and Edmund Hillary stepped out of their comfort zones, overcame fear to emerge successful and became pioneers of human civilisation.

Human beings are different from animals due to the fact that we can dream new ideas, think and plan logically, innovate and persevere to overcome fear. Like they say "Too many of us are not living our dreams because we are living our fears"!

Do we have it in us to overcome fear and emerge successful?

KYONKI...DAR KE AAGE JEET HAIN!

True Independence

On 15 August India celebrated the 70th Independence Day. Independence Day marks the Indian Republic emerging as an independent nation free from the clutches of 200 year old British Rule. Independence Day is celebrated across the country with Parades, cultural shows, *Prabhat Pheris*, etc.

However, in some areas of North East, Independence Day is marked by *Bandh* calls by various secessionist and other organisations. The days around Independence Day are marked by increased security checks harassing many travellers. Unlike other places, in Arunachal Pradesh Independence Day is celebrated with pomp and gaiety. Many people fly the national flag in front of their houses and shops. Many vehicles also fly the national flag. Sweet shops selling *Jelebis*, *Pakoras* and *Mala Rotis* spring up at many places.

Despite 70 years of independence, are we truly independent? True independence implies self reliance in food, housing, clothing for all citizens. Self reliance means non dependence on other nations for these basic requirements. True independence implies universal free education and universal free health care. It may also include essential services like free stabilised electricity, free water supply etc. It may not be too idealistic to include fundamental rights like free speech, secularism, pluralism etc.

70 years post independence, let's examine some basic figures. As per latest figures, India still has 21.9 % population below poverty line. The literacy rate of India is 74 % which is below the literacy rate of China, Sri Lanka and Myanmar. As per life expectancy, India is ranked 125 with life expectancy of 68.3 years below those of Sri Lanka, Bangladesh and Nepal. In Healthcare index, India ranks 154 below Sri Lanka and Bangladesh. According to 2016 figures of Corruption Index of Transparency International, India ranks 79th place out of 176 countries. India is also the second most unequal country in the world with the top one per cent of the population owning nearly 60% of the total wealth!

India also imports most military weapons like aircraft, ships, tanks, submarines, weapons and ammunition and thus is totally dependent on other nations.

The same figures for Arunachal Pradesh are also not so good. As per the same figures the poverty rate of Arunachal is 34.67 %. Arunachal literacy rate is 66.95 % which is third from bottom, above only Telangana and Bihar. Arunachal has also one of the highest figures of unemployment in the country with figures of about 90 per 1000. Arunachalese do not have universal free education and universal free health! These figures combined with lack of stabilised electricity and poor infrastructure like roads, water supply etc makes life of an average Arunachali harder than others.

Except for few items, Arunachal depends on other states for most of its requirements of food, clothes, groceries, pen, paper, soap, etc...almost all products!!

It is admitted that these basic figures are much higher as compared to the eighties and the nineties. However, these figures indicate that we are still lagging behind other nations and Arunachal is lagging behind other states.

How many more Independence Days would be required to achieve independence in the true sense?

SEPARATE TIME ZONE FOR NORTH EAST

Recently the Govt of India rejected the demands of North East India to have different time zone compared to the remaining parts of the country. The demand for separate time zone for North East has been popping up at frequent intervals by various political leaders, organisations and intellectuals. Comparatively, Bangladesh which is west of North East and Myanmar which is alongside North East are one hour ahead of Indian Standard Time (IST). USA has 9 Time Zones, Australia 3 Time Zones, Indonesia 3 Time Zones, Brazil 4 Time Zones! Presently IST is taken from longitude passing through Allahabad and is set at UTC plus 5:30 Hrs.

Historically India had three time zones after independence in 1947. India established IST as the official time for the whole country; however, Kolkata and Mumbai retained their own local time (known as Kolkata Time and Bombay Time) until 1948 and 1955, respectively. Presently in Assam, tea gardens follow a separate time zone, known as the *Chaibagaan* time (Tea Garden Time), which is one hour ahead of IST.

The major reason quoted for demanding different time zone was Loss of daylight hours and excess electricity usage. A different time zone would allow sunsets to take place later, allowing the citizens to better use their daylight hours. The other major reason was the effect on biological clocks of citizens. The longitudinal extremes of the country are assigned a single time zone which not only creates the loss of daylight hours but also creates problems relating to the biological clock.

India's East to West distance stretches to almost 3000 km equivalent to almost 2 Hours time difference. Therefore when it is 6 AM in Ahmedabad it is equivalent to 8 AM in Itanagar. In the Northeast, the sun rises as early as four in the morning and in winter it sets by four in the evening. Therefore in winters, offices would remain open in North East after sunset requiring lights for at least one hour. By the time government offices or educational institutions open, many daylight hours are already lost. As per calculations, advancing IST by half an hour in North East would result in saving 2.7 billion units of electricity every year.

Major reasons for refusal to grant different time zone includes chaos in Railway/Airline timings which may lead to accidents, difference in office/ bank timings, may instigate separatism etc.

Why does the Central Govt reject genuine and logical demands of North East India? By the way, the national anthem written by Rabindranath Tagore does not mention North East India at all! Therefore there was a proposal to include Brahmaputra in the National Anthem; this demand was also rejected. The way to bypass this Centrist Authoritarianism is by enacting laws in the local assemblies of the states of North East India. Recently the Chief Ministers of Assam, Tripura and Arunachal Pradesh have also issued statements supporting different time zones for North East India.

Due to different time zones, most people of North East are eating Breakfast at almost Lunch Time!

3

ABU TANI'S SPEAKING TREE

ABU TANI'S SPEAKING TREE...!

'Son Takang...you see...too much of wealth acquired easily, in a short time ultimately shortens your life...!' Abu Tani advised.

'How is that possible...Abu...I didn't understand' Takang replied.

'You have to understand the value of money...otherwise money starts controlling you' Abu Tani continued.

'But Abu...money is required for everything today...money brings position, respect and power' Takang replied.

'Yes, wealth is essential for living well...but money has many ill effects and like a Frankenstein's monster...money can gobble you up' Abu Tani continued.

'Abu...with money you can buy comforts of life...vehicles to travel in ease, good food, house for protection from vagaries of weather, stylish clothes...you can send children to reputed schools...in fact money can help treat diseases and avoid ill health' Takang said.

'Son you see...vehicle is required to travel faster and comfortably between two places...but after a while you start depending on vehicles to go everywhere, even to the corner shop...you stop walking and running...you go in vehicles to even go to the gym or go for walking!' Abu Tani continued...'your children and family also becomes dependant on vehicles...gradually you stop exercising and start collecting fat and body weight'

'Hmmm...that appears true, Abu...' Takang replied

'Money allows you to buy food for a healthy diet...but gradually you start eating meat, fish, butter, ghee etc in every meal...you start getting more calories and sugar through hard drinks and soft drinks...all this adds to your putting on weight and diseases start hitting you sooner...now a day's juvenile diabetes and obesity is commonly seen...' Abu Tani replied

'That also appears logical, Abu...' Takang nodded.

'Since you assume that money brings power and prestige you become arrogant and misbehave with other human beings like your friends, servants, children, family members...you start losing genuine friends and well wishers...' Abu Tani said.

'You start gifting your family members and children expensive items like bikes, cars, mobiles etc. You start giving them more money. As a result children learn that money is easily available and stop studying, working, exercising and gets spoilt. You may have earned your money...but your children may easily squander your money and property!' Abu Tani continued.

'Yes, I tend to agree with you, Abu...' Takang replied.

'Son...money is a double edged sword...it is a weapon to make you...or it is an evil to break you...weapon or evil depends on your understanding and utilisation of money!' Abu Tani said.

'You give smart mobiles to your children...they may use it for keeping connected and passing essential information...they may also use it for playing games, watching videos, listening to songs...it depends on the child and the grooming' Abu Tani said.

'You give laptops to you children...they may use it for doing projects, keeping connected etc...they may also use it for playing games, watching videos, listening to songs etc...it again depends on the child' Abu Tani continued

'But Abu...what explains very rich people like the Tatas, Birlas, Ambanis, Mahindras...?'

'Hmmm...good question...the only logical explanation is that these people are traditionally rich and understands the value of money...they are able to control money and thus avoid its ill effects...!' Abu Tani replied.

'Thank you, Abu...you have cleared many of my nagging questions' Takang replied.

Abu Tani concluded by saying 'Son Takang...most people run after money thinking money is the panacea for all problems...least realising that along with it, money brings many ill effects like laziness, obesity, gluttony, arrogance, hubris etc...Humans must understand how to use money...as a blessing or as a curse...!!'

ABU TANI'S SPEAKING TREE 1

'Son Takang...you are successful and rich in your generation...but the next generation is unable to match you...!' Abu Tani said.

'Hmmm...Abu, I don't understand' Takang replied.

'See...you and your contemporaries lived in remote villages, walked long distances to reach school, toiled hard to become engineers, doctors, govt officers, lecturers...' Abu Tani continued 'However, many of your children are unable to graduate and find jobs of equal standing...many of them are still struggling to stand on their own'

'I see Abu...' Takang replied.

Abu Tani said 'Your parents lived in *kutcha* houses in fur flung villages, had menial jobs or worked hard in fields as farmers to just about manage to educate you and your siblings...they did not have any resources to indulge in you and your siblings...therefore you understood the value of money and worked hard to do well in life'.

Abu Tani continued 'After you became officers and started doing well, you moved into big houses, lived in towns, started owning many vehicles, sent children to good schools and started indulging in your children...'

'You employed servants to look after your children, cook and wash for you and your children...your children depended on servants to do most things...you gave your children cars, bikes, mobiles, laptops...in the process they eventually started believing that they can afford things with parent's money...they stopped working hard to achieve better results...!'

'Abu...our children are also becoming professors, government officers, engineers, specialists doctors etc' Takang replied.

'Yes son, some children are doing well. Few parents have groomed their children well, imbibed good values and raised them to become responsible citizens. We want more of them' Abu Tani replied.

'That's right Abu, these children are making us proud...' Takang replied.

'From childhood, you learnt to wake up early, eat on time, go to office on time and sleep on time, do your own work...but many present day children wake up late, skip breakfast, eat junk food and sleep very late in the night... these erratic lifestyle is not good for their health...' Abu Tani said.

'If that is the case, what is the solution Abu?' Takang asked.

'There are no fixed solutions to this complex issue' Abu replied 'As a start, parents have to spend time with the children and talk to them... parents need to be strict with children and stop getting blackmailed into over indulgence...one way maybe is to set milestones for them...like mobile phones after Class X, laptops in college only, vehicle after getting a job etc; also parents need to set personal examples for the children'.

'I understand now Abu' Takang nodded.

'Son Takang...one of the greatest duty of parents is to ensure that their children become responsible citizens of the world and surpass their parents in all fields' Abu Tani said 'Isn't it son?'

'Yes Abu, you are right...the next generation logically should be smarter, healthier and happier!' Takang replied.

ABU TANI'S SPEAKING TREE 2

'Why is it so hot now a days, Abu?' asked Yapi

'Daughter Yapi...many actions of humans have led to extreme weather in many parts of our beloved planet' replied Abu Tani.

'Abu, if it rains, it rains continuously causing terrible floods, temperatures are rising throughout the country' Yapi said.

'Humans have caused large scale deforestation around our towns and villages. Humans have cut big trees for timber business. Even the vegetation near towns has not been spared. Vegetation has been cut in towns to create more land for buildings, roads and big projects.' Abu Tani replied.

'Today there are many vehicles emitting poisonous gases into the environment around us. Poisonous gases are emitted by generators, industries, thousands of air conditioners and refrigerators. In most cities it is difficult to breathe due to the air pollution.' Abu Tani continued.

'We are polluting our rivers...as a result many of us are drinking, bathing and washing with contaminated and polluted water. Due to pollution, contamination and deforestation, the small rivers and water sources that existed in or near our towns are drying up leading to lack of water sources.' Abu Tani continued.

'Uncontrolled fishing by using dynamite, generators and poison has led to depletion of traditional fish sources. Humans are not even allowing our fish to breed. Most birds have been exterminated by rampant use of air guns and rifles.'

'Uncontrolled deforestation has led to the extinction of many species of birds, insects and animals. Traditionally there were variety of insects and birds that used to warn humans about change of seasons, natural calamities, and unusual occurrences with their typical cries and sounds. These insects, birds and animal that used to warn us are being exterminated due to large scale deforestation' Abu Tani continued. 'These typical cries and sounds by various insects, birds and animals acted as our friends and guided our lives.'

'But Abu, we require industries, vehicles, generators, air conditioners and refrigerators to lead a comfortable life...are there any solutions from this frightening scenario, Abu?' Yapi asked.

'Though the damage to the earth's environment maybe extensive, it may still not be too late to implement changes to reverse this process. The first would be carry out large scale plantation and nurture these plantations in our towns and villages. Our rivers in towns and villages should be cleaned up and decontaminated. We have to start shifting to electric, non polluting vehicles. Rain water harvesting, good drainage systems, use of bio gas and bio fuels, solar energy etc should be encouraged and implemented.' Abu Tani continued.

'Like we have been doing for ages, we should live in consonance with nature i.e. with forests, animals, birds and insects...all have been designed for specific roles to help life on earth...'

'Daughter Yapi...do you want development at the cost of massive damage to the environment and earth?'

'No Abu, we must protect our planet...we must leave behind a healthy and liveable earth for our next generations...We owe it to our children and grand children!' Yapi replied.

ABU TANI'S SPEAKING TREE 3

'Come, all my sons...Where are you all? Techi, Hage, Take, Gamli, Kaling and Migom...come to me' Abu Tani summoned his six sons.

'I am here Abu...' Techi replied.

'Abu, I am here...' Hage replied.

'I am here Abu...' Take replied.

'Abu, I am here...' Gamli replied.

'I am here Abu...' Kaling replied.

'Abu, I am here...' Migom replied.

'My sons...how are you all? Are your lives on Earth comfortable...?' Abu Tani asked his children.

'Abu...we all are fine...we are living comfortably on Mother Earth...we and our families are happy...' Techi replied.

'Abu...we have sufficient to eat...our granaries are full and our children are healthy' Hage replied.

'Abu...we have comforts of life like houses to live in, dresses to wear, vehicles to drive' Take replied.

'Abu...we are well educated...our children are going to good schools' Gamli replied.

'Abu...we are retaining our culture, customs and traditions that you taught us' Kaling replied.

'Abu...our social life is good...we have maintained good relations with our neighbours...' Migom replied.

'Being your father, I am very happy to hear that all of you are living well on Mother Earth' Abu Tani continued. 'However, I have to ask you some questions'

'Why are so many trees being cut? Why are you killing so many animals, birds and fish? This is not the Earth Donyi Polo gave us...! I have always taught you to live in consonance with nature' Abu Tani continued.

'If Mother Earth has given so much to us, we must care for and protect whatever grows or lives on earth' Abu Tani continued.

'I can also see that some of you are picking up few wrong traits like dishonesty, stealing, cheating, cunningness, arrogance etc. My advice to you all is to correct yourself and live a life of high principles' Abu Tani continued.

'My children...you are no less than anyone...go forth and conquer the world with wisdom, research, hard work and discipline. Show the world that the sons and daughters of Abu Tani are no less than any other human being on earth' Abu Tani continued.

'You all are my sons...I love all six of you equally...but I can see that few of you are picking up fights and quarrelling with each other. There may be minor differences in each of you...but always remember that you all are blood brothers. You all speak the same language and have similar customs and traditions. My advice to you is to please cooperate with each other and live in unity. Otherwise each of you will go different ways and other people will divide and use you' Abu Tani continued.

'Remember my children united you stand and divided you fall...'

'Promise me, my children...' Abu Tani urged his children.

'As your sons and daughters, we will work hard to excel in this world and as advised by you we promise to remain united' all six children replied in a chorus.

'Yes sons...always remember we all are one...we are TANI...!' concluded Abu Tani.

Abu Tani's Speaking Tree 4

'Son Takang and daughter Yapi, how are you both? How is life on mother earth?' Abu Tani asked his children.

'Abu, life is good...we have good houses, vehicles, TVs, schools, hospitals to treat diseases...' Takang replied.

'Abu, we have good clothes to wear, beauty parlours to make up and bazaars to go shopping...' Yapi replied.

'I am happy for you both. But how about quality of life? Is your life on earth peaceful and contented?' Abu Tani asked.

'Hmmm...Abu, we are so busy with our jobs that we do not get adequate time with family members. We are laughing less and getting angry more.' Takang continued 'When we are not in office...we are either at a traffic jam or busy with mobiles/computer...it seems everyone is in a rush, irritable, short tempered and foul mouthed'.

'Abu...everyone is so busy with mobiles, computers, internet and TV that there is no time for each other. Even when we are sitting together every member of the family is busy with mobiles, busy with what's app, facebook or playing games...no one talks to one another...even my husband rarely talks to me!' Yapi complained.

'And since we hardly talk with each other, there is a communication gap between all members...parents misunderstand children...brother misunderstand sister...husbands do not understand wives and grandparents do not understand anyone...' Yapi continued.

'See children...gadgets and appliances are meant to increase your efficiency so that you can spare some quality time with near and dear ones. Computers are supposed to make working easier and faster thus affording more time for other works...internet is meant to get accurate data instantly instead of searching for hours...mobiles are supposed to give instant connectivity...it is humans that have started exploiting these gadgets in the wrong ways' Abu Tani said.

'Children...earlier your parents and grandparents lived in simple *kutcha* houses which had no locks, hardly any clothes to wear, no TVs, mobiles and computers...yet they were happy and contented. They ate what they grew...to reach places they walked or ran...they spent more time with family members and were happy and peaceful' Abu Tani continued.

'Happiness and peace is not dictated by gadgets, appliances, equipment and modernity...happiness and peace are a state of mind and under one's own control...mobiles cannot give you happiness, if used for long durations it can give you harmful radiations...computers cannot give you peace of mind, prolonged use may spoil your eye sight etc!

'Oh children...decide for yourself what kind of life do you want "A busy, well connected, well informed but hectic, unhealthy and chaotic life" OR "A slower, efficient, healthy, peaceful and contented life" Abu Tani said.

'You are right Abu...we will change our lifestyles to be more happy and contented' replied Takang and Yapi in a chorus.

4

HEROES OF 1962 INDO-CHINA WAR

HEROES OF 1962 WAR IN ARUNACHAL: BATTLE OF HENKAR 1

Many Arunachali veterans and old timers recall the 1962 Indo-Chinese conflict with fear and anger. It is a known fact that the Chinese forces entered deep into Arunachal Pradesh along many axes. The main axes of penetration by the Chinese forces were *Tawang-Bomdila-Rupa Axis, Taksing-Limeking Axis, Mechuka/Manigong-Tato Axis, Gelling-Tuting Axis* and *Kibithoo-Walong Axis*. Though the Chinese forces penetrated without major opposition in most axes, many fierce battles were fought by few units and small groups of soldiers; sometimes supported by local population. Many readers in Arunachal Pradesh and our country are not aware of these fierce battles fought by our brave soldiers; many of these brave soldiers remain unknown and unsung. In a series of articles about these localised battles of the 1962 Indo-China Conflict, the attempt is to show case these brave soldiers and their heroic exploits.

Henkar Post was located about 25 km north of Manigong in present Shi-Yomi district of Arunachal Pradesh. Major PA Rege of 11 Assam Rifles was the Officer Commanding the troops positioned at the post for the defence of Manigong valley.

On the fateful day of 24 October 1962, about 500 Chinese soldiers attacked Henkar post. Though greatly outnumbered, Henkar post with a mere strength of 100 troops fought back tenaciously. Under the leadership of Major PA Rege, the troops at Henkar post repulsed four enemy attacks. Major PA Rege and his company inflicted heavy casualties on the Chinese troops. Ultimately after fierce fighting including hand to hand combat, the Chinese troops were forced to withdraw.

Major PA Rege and his soldiers successfully blocked the advance of the enemy for considerable period, thereby keeping the lines of communication open for the main garrison. Throughout this operation, Major Rege displayed exemplary courage and leadership of highest order. It was only after the orders from higher headquarters that the company left its location to take up defences at Manigong. Major PA Rege played a pivotal role during the operation. The outstanding leadership, gallantry and complete disregard for own safety, Major PA Rege was decorated with the Vir Chakra, the third highest gallantry award of the nation. The battle of Henkar post has found its mention in the golden pages of history for repulsing four enemy attacks during the 1962 Indo-China conflict.

Heroes of 1962 War in Arunachal: Battle of Henkar 2

Many Arunachali veterans and old timers recall the 1962 Indo-Chinese conflict with fear and anger. It is a known fact that the Chinese forces entered deep into Arunachal Pradesh along many axes. The main axes of penetration by the Chinese forces were *Tawang-Bomdila-Rupa Axis*, *Taksing-Limeking Axis*, *Mechuka/Manigong-Tato Axis*, *Gelling-Tuting Axis* and *Kibithoo-Walong Axis*. Though the Chinese forces penetrated without major opposition in most axes, many fierce battles were fought by few units and small groups of soldiers; sometimes supported by local population. Many readers in Arunachal Pradesh and in our country are not aware of these fierce battles fought by our brave soldiers; many of these brave soldiers remain unknown and unsung. In the Mechuka/Manigong-Tato Axis, Chinese forces entered 50-60 km inside India and reached Tato the present District HQ of Shi Yomi district of Arunachal Pradesh.

Henkar Post was located about 25 km north of Manigong in present Shi Yomi district. Rifleman Bajiram Thapa was part of a platoon of 11 Assam Rifles with the onerous responsibility of defending Henkar post; being the main entry point to Manigong valley. The Chinese forces penetrated through *Dome La* and *Nayu La* passes and attacked Henkar post in overwhelming numbers on 24 October 1962.

Rifleman Bajiram Thapa was covering the main track leading to the post. On sight of enemy, he shot dead two advancing enemy soldiers. A burst of enemy fire wounded him in his left hand, but unrelenting, he continued firing and killed yet another enemy soldier. His courage and determination was an inspiration for the platoon and the enemy attack was repulsed after heavy exchange of fire.

However, the enemy regrouped and re-attacked with more forces. By this time the enemy had got very close and Rifleman Bajiram Thapa was wounded once again by the hail of enemy bullets. His platoon was forced to withdraw from the location without him. He was left behind wounded and without food, water and adequate clothing.

Although the Gurkha was physically wounded and isolated without support, mentally he was in full spirits. He evaded capture by the enemy by escaping away from the post undetected. Having evaded capture, hid in remote caves, survived the harsh weather, and avoided detection by enemy for many days. He was assisted by the local population in this escapade who provided him food, care and miraculously he succeeded in rejoining his platoon again!

For displaying outstanding physical, mental courage, determination with complete disregard for own safety, Rifleman Bajiram Thapa was decorated with the Vir Chakra, the third highest gallantry award of the nation. The battle of Henkar post has found its mention in the golden pages of history for repulsing four enemy attacks during the 1962 Indo-China conflict.

HEROES OF 1962 WAR IN ARUNACHAL: BATTLE OF LIMEKING

Many Arunachali veterans and old timers recall the 1962 Indo-Chinese conflict with fear and anger. It is a known fact that the Chinese forces entered deep into Arunachal Pradesh along many axes. The main axes of penetration by the Chinese forces were *Tawang-Bomdila-Rupa Axis, Taksing-Limeking Axis, Mechuka/Manigong-Tato Axis, Gelling-Tuting Axis* and *Kibithoo-Walong Axis*. Though the Chinese forces penetrated without major opposition in most axes, many fierce battles were fought by few units and small groups of soldiers; sometimes supported by local population. In the Taksing-Limeking Axis, Chinese forces entered 60-80 km inside India and overran Limeking near Daporijo, the present District HQ of Upper Subansiri district of Arunachal Pradesh.

Havildar Shere Thapa of No. 2 Jammu and Kashmir Rifles was part of a protective patrol of one platoon strength located near Rio bridge to keep a strict watch on Chinese movement and delay its advance for maximum duration. Rio bridge was the main link onwards to Limeking from Taksing. Strategically entry to Limeking would open up enemy's approach to Daporijo. On 18 November 1962, about 200 Chinese troops came in contact with the protective patrol. Havildar Shere Thapa was manning a light machine gun located at a vantage point and was covering the advance of the Chinese troops. The buddy soldier of the light machine gun detachment was seriously injured in the fire fight which commenced thereafter. Havildar Shere Thapa single headedly manned the light machine gun, occupying a well camouflaged vantage position and faced waves of Chinese assault launched one after the other. He kept on firing with his light machine gun and stopped waves of Chinese attack. He kept firing the light machine gun till he ran out of ammunition thus delaying the Chinese advance alone.

This gallant action of Havildar Shere Thapa delayed the Chinese advance for nearly 72 hrs. In this encounter seventy Chinese soldiers including a senior officer were reported to be killed. The brave action of Havildar Shere Thapa won the hearts of the locals of the area who still hold him in high esteem. Even the Chinese recognized his bravery. They buried his dead body on the spot and kept a wooden epitaph near his body with an inscription in Chinese script appreciating the fighting qualities of Havildar Shere Thapa. A memorial in the memory of Havildar Shere Thapa for his indomitable courage and supreme sacrifice was made by the locals of that area which stands near *Kete Nallah* near Limeking even today.

There are very few instances of local population building memorials for unknown soldiers with own resources. There are even rarer instances wherein the enemy recognises a soldier's bravery and leaves behind an epitaph in his honour. Though he was not decorated by the nation, such was the legend of Havildar Shere Thapa that his bravery was recognised and honoured by the enemy and the local population! The battle of Limeking has found its mention in the golden pages of our history!

HEROES OF 1962 WAR IN ARUNACHAL: BATTLE OF LAMDOLA

Many Arunachali veterans and old timers recall the 1962 Indo-Chinese Conflict with fear and anger. It is a known fact that the Chinese forces entered deep into Arunachal Pradesh along many axes. The main axes of penetration by the Chinese forces were *Tawang-Bomdila-Rupa Axis*, *Taksing-Limeking Axis*, *Mechuka/Manigong-Tato Axis*, *Gelling-Tuting Axis* and *Kibithoo-Walong Axis*. Though the Chinese forces penetrated without major opposition in most axes, many fierce battles were fought by few units and small groups of soldiers; sometimes supported by local population. Many readers in Arunachal Pradesh and in our country are not aware of these fierce battles fought by our brave soldiers; many of these brave soldiers remain unknown and unsung. In the Mechuka/ Manigong-Tato Axis, Chinese forces entered 50-60 km inside India and reached Tato the present District HQ of Shi Yomi district of Arunachal Pradesh.

Lamdola Post was located about 30 km north of Manigong in present Shi Yomi district. The post was defended by only five soldiers led by Lance Naik Hasta Bahadur of 11 Assam Rifles. The enemy forces penetrated through *Shoka La* and *Nayu La* passes and attacked Lamdola post in overwhelming numbers on 24 October 1962.

On 24 October 1962, enemy forces attacked Lamdola post. In the first wave of attack, our soldier manning the Light Machine Gun (LMG) Post was killed. Lance Naik Hasta Bahadur took over the LMG post and repulsed the enemy attack. Under his leadership, the section fought fiercely and halted the enemy advance. The enemy forces renewed their attack on the post with larger numbers. During the subsequent attacks, Lance Naik Hasta Bahadur was injured by an enemy bullet. Despite the injury, he kept firing the Light

Machine Gun and repulsed waves of attacks. He kept attacking the enemy till he ran out of bullets. Being outnumbered, finally the post was captured by the enemy forces. Lance Naik Hasta Bahadur was also captured by the enemy forces.

Although Lance Naik Hasta Bahadur was physically wounded and captured, he did not give up. With his guile and alertness, he managed to escape from enemy captivity. He survived the harsh weather by hiding in remote caves and avoided detection by the enemy. After hiding and evading th enemy for many days, being assisted by the local population in this escapade and miraculously, he succeeded in rejoining his unit!

For displaying outstanding physical, mental courage, determination with complete disregard for own safety, Lance Naik Hasta Bahadur was decorated with the Vir Chakra, the third highest gallantry award of the nation. The **Battle of Lamdola** has found its mention in the golden pages of history for repulsing four enemy attacks during the 1962 Indo-China conflict.

HEROES OF 1962 WAR IN ARUNACHAL: BATTLE OF WALONG 1

Many Arunachali veterans and old timers recall the 1962 Indo-Chinese conflict with fear and anger. It is a known fact that the Chinese forces entered deep into Arunachal Pradesh along many axes. The main axes of penetration by the Chinese forces were *Tawang-Bomdila-Rupa Axis*, *Taksing-Limeking Axis*, *Mechuka/Manigong-Tato Axis*, *Gelling-Tuting Axis* and *Kibithoo-Walong Axis*. Though the Chinese forces penetrated without major opposition in most axes, many fierce battles were fought by few units and small groups of soldiers; sometimes supported by local population. Many readers in Arunachal Pradesh and in our country are not aware of these fierce battles fought by our brave soldiers; many of these brave soldiers remain unknown and unsung. In the Walong-Kibithoo Axis, Chinese forces entered 40-50 km inside India and reached Walong in Anjaw district of Arunachal.

Unlike some other areas, many fierce battles were fought by both sides in the Walong-Kibithoo sector. Sarla Post was located about between Walong and Kibithoo in present Anjaw district. The post was defended by troops from 6 Kumaon Regiment including Naik Bahadur Singh.

On 21 October 1962, just short of midnight, the Battalion level enemy forces attacked Sarla post under the cover of Artillery and Medium Machine Gun (MMG) fire. Indian forces retaliated fiercely with 3 Inch Mortar fire and MMG fire. The enemy attack was successfully repulsed after heavy fighting. In this action about 60 enemy troops were killed.

However the enemy forces regrouped and renewed their attack on the post with larger numbers of troops. Being totally outnumbered, the Indian forces carried out a tactical withdrawal towards Walong. Naik Bahadur

Singh and his team were tasked to cover the withdrawal of the main forces. Naik Bahadur Singh and his team repulsed many waves of attacks by enemy forces till they ran out of bullets. Despite being gravely injured he and his team fought and engaged the enemy in close combat with bayonets. Being grievously injured Naik Bahadur Singh succumbed to his injuries and was martyred.

For displaying outstanding physical, mental courage, determination with complete disregard for own safety, Naik Bahadur Singh was posthumously decorated with the Vir Chakra, the third highest gallantry award of the nation. The Battle of Sarla in Walong area has found its mention in the golden pages of history during the 1962 Indo-China conflict.

HEROES OF 1962 WAR IN ARUNACHAL: BATTLE OF WALONG 2

Many Arunachali veterans and old timers recall the 1962 Indo-Chinese conflict with fear and anger. It is a known fact that the Chinese forces entered deep into Arunachal Pradesh along many axes. The main axes of penetration by the Chinese forces were *Tawang-Bomdila-Rupa Axis*, *Taksing-Limeking Axis*, *Mechuka/Manigong-Tato Axis*, *Gelling-Tuting Axis* and *Kibithu-Walong Axis*. However some fierce battles were fought in the Walong-Kibithu area of present Anjaw District. In the Walong-Kibithoo Axis, Chinese forces entered 40-50 km inside India and reached Walong.

This story is about the saga of bravery and battle craft of Lieutenant Bikram Singh in the Battle of Walong. Lt Bikram Singh commanded 120 men of the 6 Kumaon's D Company. Two intense engagements with the enemy forces were significant, as they rebuffed and severely delayed the enemy assault, so much so that the enemy had to replace an entire Regiment for failing to meet their objectives. The FIRST was at Namti Nallah in the intervening night of October 22/23, 1962. The other was at West Ridge on November 16, where he died while successfully delaying the enemy advance.

The company was holding the Ladders Post when the enemy struck in the early hours of October 22 on the MacMahon Ridge 3 km south of Kibithu. He carried out a gradual withdrawal from the area and planned a classic ambush at a small hanging bridge over Namti Nallah. Lt Bikram removed the last few planks of the hanging bridge resulting in the leading enemy soldiers falling into the river. Thereafter, with many enemy soldiers on the hanging bridge, Lt Bikram and his troops opened fire leading to over 200 enemy casualties!

The rude shock at Namti and the fierce resistance offered by Indian troops over the next few days forced the enemy to reinforce its forces with additional troops.

The second major engagement was at West Ridge, overlooking Walong ALG. On November 16, over 3000 enemy forces attacked the key position at West Ridge, held by Bikram and his Company of 100 odd soldiers. Its fall would allow the Chinese to overrun Walong. He was ordered to hold the post for half an hour. However, showing tenacity and valour, his troops held off the enemy attack for more than 3 hours. Despite being totally outnumbered, under his leadership, the men fought until all of their ammunition was exhausted and they were completely overrun. There appeared to be no survivors of the battle.

Interestingly, the resting place of Lt Bikram Singh itself was discovered 22 years later in 1986 by another army unit. In 1995, a memorial dedicated to "unknown soldiers" was erected. Another memorial plaque was erected at the battle site at Namti Plains in 2011.

For displaying outstanding physical, mental courage, determination with complete disregard for own safety, the Saga of Lt Bikram Singh in the Battle of Walong has found its mention in the golden pages of history during the 1962 Indo-China conflict.

HEROES OF **1962** WAR IN ARUNACHAL: BATTLE OF WALONG 3

Many Arunachali veterans and old timers recall the 1962 Indo-Chinese conflict with fear and anger. It is a known fact that the Chinese forces entered deep into Arunachal Pradesh along many axes. The main axes of penetration by the Chinese forces were *Tawang-Bomdila-Rupa Axis, Taksing-Limeking Axis, Mechuka/Manigong-Tato Axis, Gelling-Tuting Axis* and *Kibithoo-Walong Axis*. Though the Chinese forces penetrated without major opposition in most axes, many fierce battles were fought by few units and small groups of soldiers; sometimes supported by local population. Many readers in Arunachal Pradesh and in our country are not aware of these fierce battles fought by our brave soldiers; many of these brave soldiers remain unknown and unsung. In the Walong-Kibithoo Axis, Chinese forces entered 40-50 km inside India and reached Walong in Anjaw district of Arunachal. However, unlike some other areas, many fierce battles were fought by both sides in the Walong-Kibithoo sector.

On 24 October 1962, enemy forces attacked the posts in the Kibithoo sector which were defended by soldiers of 4 Sikh Regiment under the cover of Artillery and Medium Machine Gun (MMG) fire. Indian forces retaliated fiercely and after a period of heavy fighting which saw momentum swinging towards both sides, the enemy attack was successfully repulsed. During this intense battle many enemy troops were killed.

After a brief lull, on 27 October, the enemy forces regrouped and renewed their attack on the posts with larger numbers of troops. The Indian forces fought back fiercely and foiled successive enemy attacks. Sepoy Kewal Singh and his team fought the enemy forces fiercely till he ran out of bullets. Despite being gravely injured he and his team fitted bayonets and engaged the enemy in close combat with bayonets. Being grievously injured Sepoy Kewal Singh succumbed to his injuries and was martyred.

For displaying outstanding physical, mental courage, determination with complete disregard for own safety, Sepoy Kewal Singh was posthumously decorated with the Maha Vir Chakra, the third highest gallantry award of the nation. This Battle in Walong area has found its mention in the golden pages of history during the 1962 Indo-China conflict.

Heroes of 1962 War in Arunachal: Battle of Bum-La

Many Arunachali old timers recall the 1962 Indo-Chinese conflict with fear and anger. The Chinese forces entered deep into Arunachal Pradesh along many axes like *Taksing-Limeking, Mechuka/Manigong-Tato, Gelling-Tuting, Kibithoo-Walong Axes and the main Tawang-Bomdila-Rupa Axis*. Many readers in Arunachal Pradesh and in our country are not aware of fierce battles fought by our brave soldiers. One such story is the saga of Param Vir Chakra Subedar Joginder Singh.

On October 20, 1962, three regiments of the Chinese Army attacked the ill-prepared Indian position at Namka Chu on the MacMahon line. The Chinese then turned their attention towards the strategically important town of Tawang. The shortest approach to Tawang passed through Bum-La axis. One platoon of the 1 Sikh Regiment under Subedar Joginder Singh was manning the defences of Bum-La.

Early on 23 October, the Chinese army launched a heavy offensive on Bum-La. Supported by artillery and mortar fire, the Chinese troops attacked in three waves, each around 200 soldiers strong. Subedar Joginder and his men mowed down the first Chinese attack. Stunned by the loss of the first wave, the next wave of Chinese troops hurled themselves at the Indian soldiers, but they were dealt with similarly. However, by then, the platoon had lost half its men. Joginder had been badly wounded in the thigh but he refused to be evacuated. Though out-manned and out-gunned, the tenacious soldier was not willing to withdraw an inch and continued to fight with all he had.

Inspired by their leader's gallantry and tenacity, the platoon stubbornly held on to its ground. As the furious Chinese started their third wave of attack, Joginder himself manned a light machine-gun firing at the attackers. The enemy onslaught, however, continued to advance despite heavy losses.

When the platoon ran out of ammunition, Joginder and the remaining soldiers fixed their bayonets and unmindful of certain death, charged at the Chinese for a last-ditch attack. Shouting their battle cry '*Bole So Nihal, Sat Sri Akal*", Joginder's gallant band of soldiers fought ferociously, bayoneting scores of Chinese soldiers before they were overpowered.

After four hours of fierce fighting, a mortally wounded Joginder was taken prisoner of war. He later died in Chinese captivity. Of the 23 men who formed Joginder's platoon, only three survived - that too because they had been sent to fetch more ammunition from the main army camp.

For his dogged determination and raw courage in the face of the enemy, Subedar Joginder Singh was posthumously awarded India's highest wartime gallantry award, Param Vir Chakra. On learning that Joginder had been awarded the Param Vir Chakra, the Chinese army, in a rare mark of respect, recognised his valour in battle by repatriating his ashes with full military honours to India on May 17, 1963. The nation salutes Param Vir Chakra Subedar Joginder Singh!

Heroes of 1962 War in Arunachal: Battle of Nuranang

Many Arunachali old timers recall the 1962 Indo-Chinese conflict with fear and anger. The Chinese forces entered deep into Arunachal Pradesh along many axes like *Taksing-Limeking, Mechuka/Manigong-Tato, Gelling-Tuting, Kibithoo-Walong Axes and the main Tawang-Bomdila-Rupa Axis*. Many readers are not aware of fierce battles fought by our brave soldiers. One such story is the epic Battle of Nuranang.

During the war, 4 Garhwal Rifles was ordered to prepare delaying position at Nuranang (Now called Jaswantgarh) in the role of covering troops for the main defenses at Sela. 'A' Company was deployed left of the Sela-Jang road and was led by Second Lieutenant SN Tandon.

On 17 November 1962, the Chinese attacked with about two Infantry battalions in three waves but were beaten back due to good defensive preparation and support weapons like Light Machine Guns (LMG). However, during the fourth attack, Chinese deployed a Medium Machine Gun (MMG) within 30 metre of the Indian bunkers. As their MMG started firing, Chinese attacks commenced again. Within seconds, the situation became desperate.

Tandon sensed the gravity of situation and asked for volunteers to silence the MMG. Lance Naik Trilok Singh Negi, Rifleman Jaswant Singh Rawat and Rifleman Gopal Singh Gusain volunteered for this perilous task. They crawled to within 15 Yards of enemy MMG and with grenades and supporting gun fire from Trilok Singh, Jaswant Singh & Gopal Singh Gusain charged the Chinese. Getting close to the Chinese MMG, they lobbed their grenades and Jaswant leapt into the post, snatched the MMG from the Chinese and started running back towards the trench covered by Trilok Singh's support fire. However, Trilok Singh was hit by enemy fire. Jaswant Singh with MMG in one hand was hit by a bullet in his head as he was about to reach the trench. Gopal Singh was also wounded but managed to reach the trench, dragging the MMG. This entire action took about 15 minutes but the courage of these men changed the course of the battle. Fifth & sixth attacks by the Chinese were also repulsed. The entire operation cost the Chinese 300 dead and wounded with few losses of Garhwal rifles.

4 Garhwal Rifles was awarded Battle Honour NURANANG, the only battle honour awarded to any army unit in the 1962 war. Rifleman Jaswant Singh Rawat was awarded the Maha Vir Chakra and Lance Naik Trilok Singh Negi and Rifleman Gopal Singh Gusain were awarded Vir Chakra.

Today Jaswantgarh has become a legendary tourist spot. Locals have created a myth around the battle of Jaswantgarh, crediting the resistance and heroic action only to Jaswant Singh and two young girls, Nura and Sela, who helped him resist the Chinese. Local folklore has it that the Chinese finally captured Jaswant Singh and beheaded him, taking his head away as trophy! Such is the epic saga of Battle of Nuranang and Jaswantgarh!

5

HEROES OF ARUNACHAL & INDO-PAK CONFLICTS

Heroes of Arunachal: Hangpan Dada, Ashok Chakra (P)

This article is about the saga of bravery and gallantry of a proud son of Arunachal Pradesh, Havildar Hangpan Dada, Ashok Chakra (Posthumous). Many Indians may not know about the bravery and sacrifice of this proud son of Arunachal Pradesh.

Hangpan Dada was born on 2nd October 1979 in Borduria village of Tirap district. He was a keen sportsman and used to run several kilometres even as a child. During his young days, he saved his childhood friend from drowning in a river. Hangpan Dada joined the Army and joined the 3rd Battalion of the Parachute Regiment on 28 October 1997. After some years, he was transferred to the 4th Battalion of Assam Regiment. Later on his request, in May 2016, he was transferred to 35 Rashtriya Rifles deployed in Kupwara district, Jammu and Kashmir.

In May 2016, Havildar Dada's unit was deployed in Naugam sector in Jammu & Kashmir. On 26 May 2016, his unit had received information from intelligence sources about the presence of terrorists in the Naugam sector. A decision was taken to launch a search and destroy operation to flush out the terrorists. In the night of 26 May, Havildar Dada along with his comrades led a charge on the hiding terrorists. After reaching the suspected area, Havildar Dada along with his team spotted the movement of terrorists and launched a well coordinated attack on them. A fierce gun-battle ensued that went on for over 24 hours. Havildar Dada killed two terrorists on the spot in a swift and daring action. On seeing this, the other two terrorists fled and hid behind some boulders. Spotting the two terrorists, Havildar Dada lunged at one of them. The two were locked in hand-to-hand combat, slipping and sliding down the hill, till Havildar Dada finally neutralized him.

However, the fourth terrorist sprayed bullets into him. Ignoring his grievous wounds, he pinned down the shooter and severely injured him. The terrorist was eventually killed but Havildar Dada succumbed to his injuries and was martyred. Havildar Dada killed three terrorists in the operation single-handedly and his action led to elimination of the fourth terrorist. His action of eliminating three terrorists in an engagement at close quarters and injuring a fourth one, in disregard to his personal safety, foiled the infiltration bid and ensured the safety of his comrades.

Considering his gallant action, bravery and supreme sacrifice in the service of the nation, Havildar Hangpan Dada was awarded the Highest Peacetime Gallantry Award of the nation, the ASHOK CHAKRA posthumously.

Havildar Hangpan Dada is survived by his wife, Chasen Lowang and two children. A memorial honouring him has been erected at his village. In his honour, the Govt of Arunachal Pradesh has renamed the annual football and volleyball tournaments for Chief Minister's Trophy as Hangpan Dada Memorial Trophy.

Hangpan Dada is a Pride of Arunachal Pradesh and India.

Heroes of Arunachal: Amarveer Tape Yajo, Kirti Chakra

This article is about the saga of bravery and gallantry of a proud son of Arunachal Pradesh, Naik Tape Yajo, Kirti Chakra (Posthumous). Many Arunachalese do not know about the bravery and sacrifice of this proud son of Arunachal Pradesh.

Naik Tape Yajo, son of Shri Tamang Yajo and Smt Yappon Yajo was born on 19 August 1977 at remote Manigong in Shi Yomi district. He was a resident of Village Bogdo, Aalo and alumnus of Nehru Memorial High School, Aalo. He was a keen sportsman and wanted to serve the nation by joining the Indian Army. Naik Tape Yajo was enrolled into 1 Assam Regiment of Indian Army on 26 December 1995. He served with sincerity and distinction in the Army for twelve plus years and was promoted to the rank of Naik.

On 21 September 2008, during operations against terrorists in Jammu & Kashmir he volunteered to be the leading scout of the attacking column tasked to eliminate terrorists in Poonch Sector of Jammu & Kashmir. During the operation, terrorists attacked unexpectedly from a very close range with heavy automatic gun fire. Being an Arunachali warrior and displaying most conspicuous bravery with utter disregard for own safety, Naik Tape Yajo and his team charged the terrorists and he killed one terrorist in close combat. In the ensuing gunfight at close range, Naik Tape Yajo was wounded with bullet injury.

Despite bleeding profusely and being wounded, he charged the terrorists at close range. His bravery motivated his comrades and in the ensuing close combat, he and his team killed 3 hardcore terrorists. His gallant action led to the elimination of the terrorists without causing further damage to the nation. Being grievously injured, Naik Tape Yajo succumbed to his injuries and laid down his life on 22 September 2008.

Considering his gallant action, bravery and supreme sacrifice in the service of the nation, Naik Tape Yajo was awarded the Second Highest Peacetime Gallantry Award of the nation, the KIRTI CHAKRA posthumously. The Kirti Chakra is equivalent to the Maha Vir Chakra.

There is a stadium in Aalo named after Amarveer Tape Yajo. He is survived by his 75 Years old father, 70 Years old mother, wife, one son and two daughters. Naik Tape Yajo is a Pride of the Arunachal Pradesh and India.

Heroes of Arunachal: Lance Naik Patey Tassuk, Sena Medal & Bar (Posthumous)

Most Arunachalese know about Ashok Chakra Late Hangpan Dada. There are also many patriots and heroes from Arunachal Pradesh who have displayed extraordinary courage and bravery fighting terrorists for our nation. The heroic deeds of these Arunachalee soldiers are unknown to many readers. One such story is the story of Lance Naik Patey Tassuk, Sena Medal & Bar (Posthumous) who hails from Banderdewa, at the gateway to Arunachal Capital Itanagar. Lance Naik Patey Tassuk belonged to 17 Guards Regiment and was serving in 21 Rashtriya Rifles since 07 October 2010.

15-16 June 2011. On 15 June 2011, Lance Naik Patey Tassuk was part of a team assigned to raid a terrorist hideout in the Krumhur forest area near Kupwara in Kashmir. He and his buddy officer eliminated a foreign terrorist in the ensuing operation. Later on 16 June, during the same operation, his team was fired upon by another terrorist hiding behind a boulder. Patey Tassuk rolled in thick bushes for about 25 metre to the flank under covering fire; he crawled amidst heavy fire to within 5 metre from the terrorist and charged the terrorist. He engaged the terrorist in one-to-one fire fight and killed the terrorist. For this operation, Lance Naik Patey Tassuk was awarded his First Sena Medal (Gallantry).

25 August 2011. About 2 months later Lance Naik Patey Tassuk was detailed as scout of Ghatak platoon tracking movement of terrorists in Rajpur area of Kashmir. Leading his team at night, he observed suspicious movement of civilians at about 70 metre. He also spotted two suspicious individuals moving behind the civilians. Having ascertained that the suspicious individuals were terrorists, he allowed the civilians to cross without firing on the terrorists to avoid civilian casualties. After the civilians crossed, he challenged the terrorists and engaged the terrorists. Though the terrorists were eliminated, Patey Tassuk was hit on the head by a terrorist bullet and succumbed to his injuries. His initiative and sacrifice to avoid civilian casualties cost him his life. For this bravery, sacrifice and emulatory commitment, Lance Naik Patey Tassuk was awarded the second Sena Medal (Gallantry) posthumously.

Lance Naik Patey Tassuk was martyred defending the nation and has left behind widow Ari and two young children.

These inspirational stories about Arunachali soldiers fighting terrorists and defending the nation in faraway places must be told and narrated to the entire nation. More such stories of bravery and honour are waiting to be told. Salute to *Saheed* Patey Tassuk!!

Heroes of Arunachal: Colonel Hemonto Panging, Sena Medal & Bar

Most Arunachalese know about Ashok Chakra Late Hangpan Dada. There are also many patriots and heroes from Arunachal Pradesh who have displayed extraordinary courage and bravery fighting terrorists for our nation. The heroic deeds of these Arunachalee soldiers are unknown to many readers. One such story is the story of Colonel Hemonto Panging, Sena Medal & Bar who hails from Namsing Village near Pasighat in East Siang District of Arunachal Pradesh. He has accounted for the elimination of countless terrorists over a period of 10 years in Jammu & Kashmir. A couple of notable operations are narrated below.

1993. In the mountains of Doda in Jammu & Kashmir, above the river Chenab, 20-25 Terrorists were operating from a hideout in the mountains. On getting information about them, Indian Army launched operations. While the main body launched operations from below, a small team led by Captain Hemonto Panging infiltrated behind the terrorists and attacked the terrorists. Rushing the terrorists, Captain H Panging and his team shot down 3 Terrorists in the initial onslaught. On being further attacked, the remaining terrorists jumped into a nearby gorge. Captain H Panging and his team ran after the terrorists into the gorge and shot down another 7 Terrorists which included two foreign terrorists. In 1993 this operation was a major success for the Army in Doda. For this operation, Capt Hemonto Panging was awarded his First Sena Medal (Gallantry).

1997. In a retaliatory cross border action Major Hemonto Panging led a team of Indian Army Special Forces tasked to neutralise terrorists in a Launch Pad adjacent to a village in Pakistan Occupied Kashmir (POK). The team crossed the Line of Control and attacked the Launch Pad located about 4-5 km inside POK. In this night operation, the Special Forces team neutralised about 20 Terrorists. The entire operation lasted about one hour. For this daring cross border operation inside enemy territory, Major Hemonto Panging was awarded the second Sena Medal (Gallantry).

1997. Major Hemonto was also awarded Commendation by Chief of Army Staff for capturing the First Shoulder Fired Surface-to-Air Missile held by terrorists at Bafliaz in Kashmir. During this operation Major H Panging and his team also killed 5 Terrorists thereby preventing the possible Surface-to-Air Missile strike on own aircraft. His team also suffered one fatal casualty and two of his jawans were injured in this operation.

These inspirational stories about Arunachali soldiers fighting terrorists and defending the nation in faraway places must be told and narrated to the entire nation. More such stories of bravery and honour are waiting to be told.

Pakistan & Abhinandan

Recent few days have seen some tense moments involving two neighbours, India and Pakistan. India and Pakistan has fought three wars in 1948, 1965 and 1971. Both countries have been involved in escalatory armed conflicts during Kargil Operations in 1999, Operation Parakram in 2001-02 and after the Mumbai terror attacks of 2008. Presently we are again in the midst of another escalatory conflict.

The trigger was the deadly, dastardly suicide attack on a CRPF convoy in Pulwama on 14 February 2019 which killed 40 CRPF personnel. The central leadership was forced to act. India struck back with vengeance on 26 February using Indian Air Force fighter aircraft to hit Terrorist Camps in Pakistan Occupied Kashmir (POK) and inside Pakistan. This was the first time the Air Force was used to strike at targets inside POK and Pakistan hitting terrorist camps at Balakot, Muzaffarabad and Chakothi areas with Precision Guided Bombs.

The next day, the Pakistani Air Force attempted to counter attack using about 24 F-16 aircraft. The Pakistani aircraft were intercepted and chased back by Indian Air Force (IAF) Fighter aircraft. In the ensuing dog fight, one Pakistani F-16 aircraft was shot down and IAF lost one Mig-21 Bison aircraft to Surface-to-Air missile. The pilot of the Mig-21 Bison aircraft Wing Commander Abhinandan ejected (parachuted) from the aircraft and landed in POK. He was rescued by the Pakistan Army after being mobbed and attacked by a frenzied mob. The videos of Abhinandan being beaten, being interrogated and questioned in Pakistan were leaked and went viral in the social media. Overnight Abhinandan became a hero and the nation prayed for his recovery. Succumbing to international pressure and pressure from India Wing Commander Abhinandan was repatriated to India through the Wagah border on 01 March 2019. I served with Abhinandan and his father (Air Marshal Varthaman Rtd) for many years and I salute the bravery and pugnacity of Wing Commander Abhinandan.

There are two critical points to ponder over these engagements over the last few days. First is the news that an F-16 aircraft was shot down by a Mig-21 Bison aircraft. If true, this would be a major achievement for the Indian Air Force to shoot down an advanced aircraft like F-16 with a much older aircraft like Mig-21 Bison aircraft. It indicates the high levels of training and professionalism of IAF Pilots!

The second was that after the Mumbai terror attacks of 2008, when I was commanding a Sukhoi-30MKI Squadron, our Squadron was activated and deployed for over a month in North India. After deployment, we trained and prepared for similar attacks on terrorist camps inside POK. If cleared from the central leadership, similar surgical strikes on terrorist camps inside POK could have been carried out. If such strikes were carried out in 2008, maybe many innocent Indian lives lost to cross border terrorism could have been saved. The go ahead from the central leadership never came in 2008!

India has been continuously bled by cross border terrorism. We need a strong leadership to stop these terrorist acts. Maybe, these strikes on terrorist camps inside POK is the first step towards stopping these cross border terrorist attacks!! A new beginning indeed!

F-16 & Mɪɢ-21
Dᴏɢꜰɪɢʜᴛ ᴏᴠᴇʀ Pᴀᴋɪꜱᴛᴀɴ

India and Pakistan has fought three wars in 1948, 1965 and 1971. Both countries have been involved in escalatory armed conflicts during Kargil Operations in 1999, Operation Parakram in 2001-02 and after the Mumbai terror attacks of 2008. There is another escalatory conflict brewing between both countries.

There has been a quantum jump in cross border terrorism in Jammu & Kashmir (J&K). The number of terrorist incidents in J&K has jumped 177 percent in the past five years. A total of 1315 people were killed in the state between 2014 and 2018 due to terrorism including 138 civilians, 339 security personnel and 838 terrorists. In last 5 years, J&K saw 93% rise in death of security personnel in terror attacks.

Despite increase in terror acts, India traditionally prefers a laid back stance trying to solve matters diplomatically and by deploying more security personnel to protect own areas and assets. India has always avoided intensification of armed conflict fearing escalation into a full fledged war between two nuclear armed neighbours. However, Pakistan has never feared escalation and kept supporting cross border terrorism.

The trigger for retaliatory action was the dastardly attack on a CRPF convoy in Pulwama on 14 February 2019 which killed 40 CRPF personnel. India struck back with vengeance on 26 February using Indian Air Force fighter (IAF) aircraft to hit Terrorist Camps inside Pakistan. This was the first time the Air Force was used to strike at targets inside Pakistan hitting terrorist camps at Balakot, Muzaffarabad and Chakothi areas with Precision Guided Bombs.

The next day, Pakistan attempted to counter attack using about 24 F-16 aircraft. The Pakistani aircraft were intercepted and chased back by IAF Fighter aircraft. In the ensuing dog fight, one Pakistani F-16 aircraft was shot down and IAF lost one Mig-21 Bison aircraft. The pilot of the Bison aircraft Wing Commander Abhinandan ejected (parachuted) from the aircraft and landed in POK. He was rescued by the Pakistan Army after being mobbed and attacked by a frenzied mob. Succumbing to international pressure and pressure from India, Wing Commander Abhinandan was repatriated to India through the Wagah border on 01 March 2019.

What is not known to most people is that the initial reports emanating from Pakistan was that two Indian pilots were captured. What is now emerging is that the so called 'Other Pilot' was Wing Commander Shahzaz-ud-Din, the Pakistani F-16 Pilot who was shot down by Abhinandan. The tragic part was that after parachuting and landing in Pakistan, Wing Commander Shahzaz-ud-Din was lynched by the frenzied Pakistani mob thinking he was an Indian Pilot! A tragic case of mistaken identity due to Fog of War!!

India has been continuously bled by cross border terrorism. As a sovereign nation, we cannot keep bleeding continuously without hitting back. We must hit back in our own terms by our own choosing. These attacks on terrorist camps deep inside Pakistan are the assertion of a New & Powerful India!

6

INDO-CHINA RELATIONS, STRATEGY & SECURITY SCENARIO

History of McMahon Line: Bogus Chinese Claims

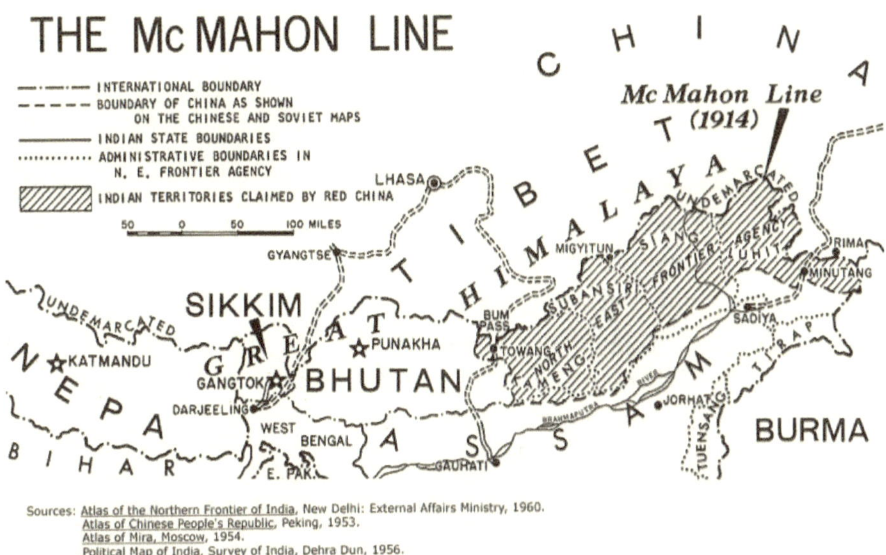

Sources: <u>Atlas of the Northern Frontier of India</u>, New Delhi: External Affairs Ministry, 1960.
<u>Atlas of Chinese People's Republic</u>, Peking, 1953.
<u>Atlas of Mira</u>, Moscow, 1954.
<u>Political Map of India</u>, Survey of India, Dehra Dun, 1956.

India & China has an acrimonious relationship over last 60 Years. The major conflict was the Indo-China war of 1962 where Chinese forces entered almost 100 km inside India. There have been regular clashes at NathuLa in 1967, Sumdorong Chu in 1987, the 73 Day Doklam confrontation in 2017, Chinese incursions in Asaphila, Tuting and Chaklagam areas of Arunachal in 2017-2018 and the recent Indo-China conflict at Pangong Tso lake and Galwan Valley in Ladakh. Tense situation exists all along the Indo-China border.

Chinese still claim Arunachal Pradesh as 'Southern Tibet' and issues stapled visas to Arunachal citizens. They object to visits by senior Indian officials, Ministers to Arunachal and uses rivers originating in China to arm twist India. The source of all these conflicts is the non-acceptance of

McMahon Line which demarcates the Indo-China border along Arunachal Pradesh.

The McMahon Line demarcates the eastern border between India and China. About 890 km in length, the McMahon Line followed the watershed principle and runs along the highest ridges of these eastern Himalayan ranges running from east of Bhutan to the tri-junction of India, China and Myanmar.

The McMahon line was created during the Shimla Agreement of 1914. The British Indian representative was Henry McMahon, then Secretary in the Indian Foreign Department. The Tibetan representative was Lama Lonchen Shatra and Chinese representative was diplomat named Ivan Chen. After almost a year of negotiations, the McMahon line was initially presented on 22 April 1914 along with an attached map. On 25 April 1914, the Chinese submitted a memorandum with number of objections to the boundaries between Inner Tibet & Outer Tibet and Inner Tibet & China. There were no objections between Tibet & India! Thereafter on 27 April 1914 the Chinese representative initialled both the documents and the map without any objections. However, the actual agreement documents were kept secret till 1937 when the McMahon line was first published in a Survey of India Map. In the western sector the border in the Ladakh and Aksai Chin area was laid by the Macartney-MacDonald line.

If the Chinese representative had no objections to the border between Tibet & India and have initialled the documents & map during Shimla agreement of 1914, why are the Chinese still claiming Arunachal as 'Southern Tibet'! This claim is bogus, hegemonic and not supported by documents & facts.

Having studied Chinese language and hailing from Arunachal Pradesh, it may be stated that people of Arunachal Pradesh comprising of many tribes are culturally, traditionally, linguistically different from Chinese.

Considering all these historical facts, Indian govt must run a campaign to rebut the Chinese claims amongst major nations of the world. The other way to counter the bogus Chinese claims over Arunachal Pradesh is by putting up prominent voices from Arunachal itself among the major world & national media. Time to call the Chinese bluster!!

Indo-China Doklam Standoff

The Doklam standoff between India, Bhutan and China started on 16 June 2017 and the face off continued for after 71 days! The Doklam plateau is located at the tri-junction of India, Bhutan and China near the Sikkim border. Doklam is a disputed area between Bhutan and China. India's intervention is due to the 1949 Indo-Bhutan friendship treaty. The 1949 treaty has recently been superseded by the Indo-Bhutan Friendship Treaty of 2007. The issue has been on the boil with allegations and counter allegations from both sides.

India shares 4000 km border with China. For decades there have been many border disputes along this border. The major disputes are in Kashmir, Sikkim and Arunachal Pradesh. There are smaller issues in Uttarkhand and Himachal Pradesh. In Kashmir, 38000 square km of Indian claimed territory in Aksai Chin is already under Chinese control. China and Pakistan are building strategically significant China-Pakistan Economic Corridor which links Xinjiang province of China and Gwadar port in Pakistan. A major portion of the road passes through northern Kashmir and Pakistan Occupied Kashmir. In the eastern sector China has been claiming majority of Arunachal Pradesh as its territory calling it Southern Tibet. And now, the Doklam standoff in the Sikkim-Bhutan-China tri-junction is re-surfacing. Readers may recall that Sikkim was a separate Kingdom and joined India only in 1975 after a request by the Sikkim Govt and a referendum.

China cannot be compared with Pakistan. China is major world power with very robust economy and very large, motivated military. Though China also has many disputes with other nations like Vietnam, Philippines, Japan, Taiwan etc, China has a robust indigenous military industry and manufactures majority of its aircraft, ships, submarines, tanks, weapons and ammunition. India imports majority of its aircraft, ships, submarines, tanks, weapons, ammunition and is dependent on other nations for weapons and ammunition.

India and China has already fought one war in 1962. Many rivers of Arunachal Pradesh and India originate in China. Strategists and policy makers should understand that China is a different kettle of fish! It is rhetoric based on hubris when the Indian Army chief announced recently that Indian army can handle a two and half front war. Even the mainstream India media is playing a jingoistic role adding salt to the fire.

The rhetorical statements by senior officials and politicians needs to be moderated. The dispute needs to be resolved by diplomatic methods. Any war will put back both India and China by at least 20 years. Historically, there is a tendency to look down at the Chinese. Even in 1962, India followed a Forward Policy leading to disastrous consequences. It seems the present leadership is again adopting a Forward Policy without adequate soul searching about own capabilities. As a nation, we cannot base our policies depending on claims of support by other nations. History shows that most supporting nations will not commit their forces in case of an actual conflict. It is imperative to have the capability and strength to fight and win our own battles.

In Arthashastra, our great strategist Chanakya stated the Mandala concept in 300 BC that two neighbours can never be friends! He also gave many ways of resolving conflicts. Our leadership also needs to adopt and follow some Chanakya Niti! Unlike places like Delhi, Mumbai and Kolkata, Arunachal Pradesh is a border state and would be the battleground state. Some veteran Arunachalese who have experienced the scary and bad times of 1962 are still alive. The national leadership needs to understand that Arunachal may be the battle ground, but the bigger weapons will fall some place deeper! Belonging to a border state, Arunachalese need to be more circumspect and pragmatic. War occurs when diplomacy fails. Time for some genuine Hindi-Chini Bhai-Bhai!!

STRATEGIC IMPORTANCE OF ARUNACHAL...!

Most states of India do not share border with any other country. Some states share borders with one country, a few share borders with two countries. Arunachal Pradesh is the only state in India to share borders with three countries. Arunachal shares 160 km border with Bhutan, 440 km with Myanmar and 1030 km with China.

About 95 % of Arunachal consists of high mountains and hill ranges. Up to the eastern tip of Arunachal the mountains are a part of the Himalayan ranges. In the south, the hills are part of the Patkai range. The terrain in these Himalayan ranges consists of steep mountains, deep ravines, gorges, dense jungles and turbulent rivers. The average height of these mountains ranges from few 1,000 feet to over 15,000 feet along the northern borders. Therefore Arunachal acts as a natural barrier towards the north and east.

The Tibetan plateau lies to the north and east of Arunachal. The general elevation of the terrain along the border with Arunachal ranges from 10,000 feet to over 15,000 feet. The area is marked by desolate and arid terrain without much vegetation. At these altitudes, due to less atmospheric oxygen levels, human beings require extensive acclimatisation and training to sustain even moderate levels of activity. The desolate and arid terrain makes it difficult and cost intensive for construction of many infrastructures like roads, railway, airfields, bridges etc.

Entry into Arunachal from the North and East is possible only through few passes dispersed along the mountain ranges. It is through these passes that the Chinese forces entered into Arunachal India in 1962. If these few passes are properly defended, it would be difficult for foot soldiers and supporting vehicles to gain entry into the region on a large scale. Therefore Arunachal with its imposing mountains and rough terrain constitutes a natural barrier for the Assam Valley.

If Arunachal is overrun, the Assam Valley will be exposed and there would be easy access to other parts of India.

Due to its many rapid flowing rivers, Arunachal is a source of tremendous Hydro power. It is estimated that Arunachal Pradesh has a hydropower potential of more than 50,000 megawatts (MW). It is estimated that this hydropower potential is capable of generating electricity to supply entire north India! Arunachal is also rich in mineral deposits like coal, limestone, dolomite etc. The state is also rich in rare flora and fauna. Access to these inherent capabilities cannot be frittered away by any nation.

Considering the strategic importance of Arunachal Pradesh, the nation must invest in developing and defending the state. The first step would be the identification of the few passes which allows entry into Arunachal from the North and East. These vital passes need to be strengthened and defended with vigour and urgency. This may be followed up with planning and building strategic infrastructure like all weather roads, Bridges, Railways, Airports etc to support these important defensive points. The hydro power potential of the state needs to be harnessed by building suitable dams. China has already commissioned a 510 MW dam over the Brahmaputra at Zangmu. Two more dams are under construction over the Brahmaputra in Tibet. We are debating, discussing and obstructing the construction of big dams. China is busy constructing dams!!

It is high time that we highlight the strategic importance of Arunachal Pradesh. Once the national leadership and we ourselves realise this strategic importance of our state, we will take off on the path of development and stability.

CHINESE CHECKERS: ARM TWISTING WITH RIVERS

The pollution of the Siang / Brahmaputra river has continued unabated for the last few years. Oily, mucky, slurried water is flowing down the river with increased turbidity and pollution. This flow of polluted and contaminated water has potential to seriously affect the lives and livelihood of millions of people living in Siang/ Brahmaputra Belt and Bangladesh. This contaminated and polluted water will also affect the entire ecosystem of the region including flora and fauna. Since many animals like cattle, buffalo, wild animals, birds etc are dependent on this river; it will have a major impact on livestock, aquatic life, migratory birds, wild life etc.

The contamination of the Siang/Brahmaputra has been reported in most media of North East India. A few Members of Parliament and political leaders have also raised this issue. However, busy with the Gujarat and Himachal Elections, the mainstream media has paid lip service to this serious issue.

It seems most crisis of our region emanates from China. There is a history of conflicts with our northern neighbour. Everyone knows about the Indo-China conflict of 1962 where the Chinese forces entered almost 100 km inside Indian Territory. There have been many border violations and skirmishes like *Sumdorong Chu* incident in 1987. Readers may recollect the flash floods which occurred in Arunachal Pradesh in 2000. These floods happened without rains in the area and were termed as the 'China floods' with many lives/ livestock being lost and many areas washed away. It was later revealed the flash floods were caused by collapse of a natural dam in Tibet. This was followed by the 71 Day 'Eyeball to Eyeball' confrontation over Doklam a few years ago.

China has already commissioned one 510 MW dam over the *Yarlung Tsangpo* at *Zangmu*. Three more dams are under construction at *Dagu, Jiexu* and *Jiacha*. There were also reports that China is planning a 1000 km long tunnel to divert the waters of the *Yarlung Tsangpo* to the arid region of Xinjiang.

And now we are faced with this issue of contamination of the Siang/ Brahmaputra. If the contamination and pollution of the Siang/ Brahmaputra continues for prolonged period, it would affect the lives and livelihood of humans, animals, birds and affect the entire ecosystem of the area. Many opine that it would be worse than war; almost akin to slow poisoning.

Some theories are propounding that the contamination and pollution of the Siang/ Brahmaputra is caused due to landslides caused by a series of Earthquakes in Tibet. However, the type of oily, mucky, slurried water composition may indicate contamination of the Siang/ Brahmaputra due to some massive construction work in Tibet.

Rivers are international property and belong to all citizens of the area through which it flows. Right to river water is one of the most fundamental universal rights and cannot be denied. Presently there is no water treaty between India and China. The Govt must initiate steps for a water treaty with China at the earliest.

On the flip side, if China considers Arunachal Pradesh as their territory, why should they contaminate Siang River?

Why so many problems with China? In case of any conflict with China it would directly affect Arunachal and Assam. Can we do something about it? Is anyone seriously interested?

CHECKMATING CHINA

India & China has a tense relationship over last 60 Years. Chinese forces entered deep into India during the Indo-China war of 1962. There have been frequent clashes along the Indo-China border ending with the recent violent conflict at Galwan Valley in June which resulted in 20 Indians soldiers and 40 plus Chinese soldiers killed. There are also cases of China arm twisting downstream countries by suddenly releasing water or restricting water flow along rivers originating in Tibet like Yarlung Tsangpo or Siang.

China is a major world power with the largest military of the world & is the second largest economy in the world. China's defence budget is four times India's defence budget and military infrastructure is better developed in Chinese side.

How should India tackle China in the long term? The first step would be for India to become economically strong with a robust indigenous manufacturing sector including defence manufacturing. To boost the local economy entrepreneurship, start ups and ease of doing business must be strictly promoted, supported in letter & spirit. Clearances and permissions for industries, services must be simplified & fast tracked. Need of the hour is a truly Single Window Clearance system. Presently there are numerous windows and complex system of clearances and permissions. There should be a separate ministry for Ease of Doing Business at Centre & States.

A lead has been taken with innovative policies like *Start Up India, Stand Up India, Make In India* etc. These innovative schemes need to be strengthened & implementation monitored at ground level. The other ways of boosting indigenous manufacturing is by investing in Research & Development to match contemporary technology. Another is to introduce easing parameters like Tax Holidays, Power Connections, Power/Transport Subsidies etc. Additional way of supporting indigenous manufacturing is by a policy of preferential pricing & preferential buying as announced recently as *Vocal for Local*. In must be made compulsory for all Govt departments, Govt supported institutions to procure from local manufacturers.

No nation can aspire to become a super power without producing own weapons and weapon platforms. India must open up defence production to the private sector. Presently most weapons & weapon platforms are imported from other countries. India must aim to manufacture own fighter aircraft, tanks, ships, rifles, bombs, missiles etc.

In the meantime critical infrastructure like roads, bridges, railways, airports must be developed along border areas. These will allow rapid mobilisation whenever required. The other critical infrastructures include Hardened Aircraft Shelters at Air Bases, Underground Command & Control Posts, Ammunition depots & Petroleum depots at key areas.

Covid-19 Pandemic & the recent Galwan Valley conflict are major lessons for India. India must focus on becoming a major economic power and manufacturing hub in the next few years & decades! This maybe the only guaranteed way of tackling China or any other hostile power in the near future!! Do you agree?

INFRASTRUCTURE TO CHECKMATE CHINA

China is a major world power with the largest military of the world & the second largest economy in the world. China's defence budget is four times India's defence budget and military infrastructure is better developed on Chinese side. India & China has a tense relationship over last 60 Years including a major war in 1962. There have been regular clashes ending with the recent violent conflict at Galwan Valley. China also resorts to arm twisting downstream countries by controlling water flow along rivers like Siang/Brahmaputra.

To tackle China in the long term one major step is to urgently boost infrastructure like roads, bridges, railways, airports and military infrastructure along border areas. Good roads, railways will allow rapid mobilisation whenever required. The other critical infrastructures include Hardened Aircraft Shelters (HAS) at Air Bases, Underground Command & Control Posts (C2), Ammunition & Petroleum depots at key areas.

The infrastructure on Chinese side is well developed including all weather roads, dams, railways which allow mobilisation of large forces in short time. The same level of development is lacking on our side. Strategic roads like Tezpur-Tawang road are still under construction for last 50 plus years! Similarly roads along Likabali-Daporijo-Taksing, Aalo-Mechuka/ Manigong, Pasighat-Tuting, Tezu-Walong-Kibithoo and Trans-Arunachal Highway are still being constructed and are not all weather roads. Many key bridges cannot take heavy vehicles. Although the road/bridges infrastructure has improved a lot during the last few years like Bogibeel Road/ Rail bridge over Brahmaputra, 9.15 km Sadiya bridge, 6.5 km Bomjir bridge, Sisirri bridge etc. Advanced Landing Grounds have also been constructed at Pasighat, Ziro, Mechuka, Aalo, Tuting, Walong.

Most air bases in North East lack HAS to protect our fighter aircraft. Lack of HAS would make our aircraft very vulnerable to aerial attack. Similarly key bases in North East lack well protected underground structures for C2 centres and key installations. These vital infrastructures can easily be targeted by enemy forces with bombs/ missiles.

Another key challenge is lack of adequate Ammunition and POL Depots north of the Brahmaputra. The few bridges over the Brahmaputra would be prime targets for the enemy. In case of destruction of these bridges, there would be acute shortage of large amounts of ammunition, bombs, missiles, POL required to sustain large scale military operations.

The other critical area is the few bridges in the Chicken Neck area near Siliguri corridor in north Bengal that connect North East with mainland. These few important Railway/ road bridges over the Teesta river are the only connection with the mainland. These critical bridges need to be protected or made underground below the river!

It is also perplexing that HQ of Army Corps responsible for Arunachal is based deep inside at Dimapur! To tackle a powerful adversary like China, we must invest in robust strategic infrastructure along the border to support large scale military operations. The long term neglect of military and strategic infrastructure in North East needs to be reversed and expedited. 1962 should not be repeated!!

Atmanirbhar Bharat to Checkmate China

China is a major world power with the largest military of the world & the second largest economy in the world. China's defence budget is four times India's defence budget. India & China has a tense relationship over last 60 Years including a major war in 1962. There have been regular clashes ending with the recent violent conflict at Galwan Valley.

To tackle China in the long term one major step would be for India to become economically strong with a robust indigenous manufacturing sector including defence manufacturing. To boost the local economy entrepreneurship, start ups and ease of doing business must be promoted and supported in letter & spirit. A lead has been taken with innovative policies like *Start Up India, Make In India, Act East Policy* etc. These innovative schemes need to be strengthened & implementation monitored at ground level.

Everything boils down to '*Ease of Doing Business*'. To simplify ease of doing business the requirements to start a business or industry like paperwork, permissions and bureaucratic procedures must be simplified & reduced. Other is to make the process of starting any business or industry through a Single Window. Presently there are numerous windows and complex system of clearances & permissions. Clearances for industries, businesses must be simplified & fast tracked. In fact there should be a separate ministry or department for Ease of Doing Business at Centre & States. There is also a need to introduce easing parameters like Tax Holidays, Power Connections, Power/Transport Subsidies, easy land allotment, soft loans etc.

Additional way of supporting indigenous manufacturing is by a policy of preferential pricing & preferential buying as announced recently as *Vocal for Local*. In must be made compulsory for all Govt departments, Govt supported institutions to procure from local manufacturers. This *Vocal for Local* is especially applicable to North East and Arunachal as there are negligible industries in the region. It is extremely difficult for local industries to compete with products from mainland due lack of supporting ecosystem & competition in volume. Covid-19 pandemic was a big lesson for this region as there were no manufacturers of PPEs, Sanitisers, Masks in the region! In fact many states imported PPEs and Covid Testing Kits from China!

No nation can aspire to become a major power without producing own weapons and weapon platforms. India must open up defence production to the private sector and invest in Research & Development to match contemporary technology. Presently most weapons & weapon platforms are imported from other countries including basic rifles for soldiers! We must aim to manufacture own fighter aircraft, tanks, ships, rifles, bombs, missiles etc.

Covid-19 Pandemic & the recent Galwan Valley conflict are major lessons for India. India must focus on becoming a major economic power and manufacturing hub in the next few years & decades! This maybe the only guaranteed way of tackling China in the near future! *Vocal for Local* must be promoted and supported!

Sino-India Conflict: No War Please

India & China has an acrimonious relationship over last 60 Years. The major conflict was the Indo-China war of 1962 where Chinese forces entered almost 100 km inside India. There have been regular clashes at NathuLa in Sikkim in 1967, in 1987 at Sumdorong Chu in Arunachal, the 73 Day Doklam confrontation in 2017, Chinese incursions in Asaphila, Tuting and Chaklagam areas of Arunachal Pradesh in 2017-2018.

Recently Indo-China conflict flared up in the last few months at Pangong Tso lake in Ladakh, North Sikkim and violent clashes at Galwan Valley during night of 15/16 Jun which resulted in 20 Indians soldiers and 40 plus Chinese soldiers killed. Tense situation exists all along the Indo-China border. Amidst a national movement for boycott of Chinese products & applications, the electronic & social media is full of shrill nationalist anti-China rhetoric. The moderate, pacifying voices & opinions are being subdued by warmongering, hardliner opinions.

China is a major world power with the largest military of the world & is the second largest economy in the world. China's defence budget is four times India's defence budget and military infrastructure is better developed in Chinese side. Both nations are major nuclear powers armed with many ballistic missiles. A major Indo-China conflict would be disastrous for both nations. A brief comparison of military forces of both nations is tabulated below:-

Subject	India	China
Active Military Personnel	14,44,000	21,83,000
Defence Budget	$ 66.9 Billion	$ 237 Billion
Total Combat Aircraft	2,123	3,210
Combat Aircraft	538	1232
Helicopters	722	911
Tanks	4200	13000
Armoured Vehicles	3000	40000
Artillery Guns	4295	7400
Naval Ships	285	777
Aircraft Carriers	1	2
Submarines	16	74
Border Infrastructure	Poor	Well Developed

While both sides claim & counter claim military superiority, many experts' opine that both nation are major powers and any major conflict will lead to loss of thousands of lives & massive property loss on both sides combined with uncountable misery & suffering. Avoiding a major conflict is more relevant due to the ongoing Covid-19 pandemic wherein both India & China are affected with millions losing jobs & economies in recession. A major Indo-China conflict should be avoided by tactful diplomacy. The options for India are to mobilise world opinion against Chinese aggression and hope that major world powers give us physical & moral support. The USA & allies must keep its forces deployed in South China Sea to keep major portion of Chinese forces occupied in the region.

We in Arunachal & Assam are directly affected since the battleground would be here! We should follow the teachings of our own Chanakya and practice some Chanakya Niti to avoid a war! Chanakya Niti dictates that we counter China with economic boycott and diplomacy. War must be the last option only after all other ways are ruled out!! All Arunachalese would agree that repeat of 1962 must be avoided!!

7

HISTORICAL LEGENDS

NAMAMI BRAHMAPUTRA...WHAT ABOUT SIANG...?

Historically Brahmaputra is supposed to be one of the most important rivers of India. In Sanskrit, Brahmaputra means "Son of Lord Brahma". Therefore amongst most rivers in the Indian subcontinent which have female names, this river has a rare male name. Brahmaputra is also one of the longest rivers in India.

Originating in the *Angsi glacier* near Mansorvar lake in Tibet, the Brahmaputra has different names in different nations. In Tibet and China, where it has the longest stretch, it is called as the *Yarlung Tsangpo*. The river carries out a massive U-Turn at Namcha Barwa and enters India through Arunachal Pradesh. In Arunachal Pradesh it is called as the *Siang*. The *Siang* river enters Assam south of Pasighat along the longitude of Tinsukia town, where it is joined by the Dibang river and the Lohit rivers. After flowing through Assam, the river flows into Bangladesh. In Bangladesh, the river is called *Jamuna*, *Padma* and *Meghna* before flowing into the Bay of Bengal.

In fact the Bodos, who are considered by many as the original inhabitants of the Brahmaputra valley call the river as the *"Burlung-Buthur"*. In many of their songs and writings the Brahmaputra is referred to frequently as the *"Burlung-Buthur"*.

The Brahmaputra's upper course was long unknown, and its identity with the *Yarlung Tsangpo* was only established by British led explorations in 1884-86. Before this discovery, in the plains of Assam the *Lohit* river was mistaken as the Brahmaputra for ages. There are still many songs and references referring to the Brahmaputra as *Lohit* in Assam.

Recently, Assam conducted the so called biggest river festival of India called *"Namami Brahmaputra"* meaning in Sanskrit "Obeisance to the

Brahmaputra". It was celebrated across 21 districts of Assam along the Brahmaputra in its entire stretch from Sadiya to Dhubri. However, Sadiya is situated on the banks of the *Lohit* river and not Brahmaputra. Till today many news items cover the soon to be completed longest river bridge of India at Sadiya as 'Over the Brahmaputra'! A few scholars also suggest that *Parsuram Kund* should actually be located on the Siang!!

The *Siang* river is also revered in Arunachal Pradesh. The *Siang* and its tributaries affect the livelihood of lakhs of people in central Arunachal before flowing into Assam. In fact there are five districts in Arunachal Pradesh bearing the name *Siang*.

It seems that that the great river Brahmaputra owes its greatness and legacy only in the plains of Assam. In Tibet, Arunachal Pradesh and Bangladesh the river is known by different names. Since a river flows continuously and belongs to everyone habitating the area through which it flows, can we initiate a *"Festival of Siang"* also in the same scale as *"Namami Brahmaputra"*? After all, only after passing through Arunachal Pradesh as *Siang*, the river is known as *Brahmaputra!!*

PARSHURAM KUND/BRAHMA KUND OR SIANG KUND?

As per Arunachal Tourism website and Wikipedia, *Parshuram Kund* is a Hindu pilgrimage centre situated on the Lohit river about 21 Km from Tezu. Many sources also locate Parshuram Kund on the banks of the Brahmaputra River. Parshuram Kund is also known as *Brahmakund*.

As per mythological legend, it is said that on being asked by his father, Parshuram killed his mother Renuka with an axe. The handle of the axe however clung to his hand. He was told that the only way to wash off his sin was by taking a dip in the Brahma Kund. Only then would the axe stuck to his hand drop. The spot where the axe dropped from his hand came to be known as Parshuram Kund. The site of Parashuram Kund was established by a Sadhu in the 18th century. In 1950 the old site was completely destroyed by the earthquake that hit North East India. Thousands of devotees take a holy dip in its water to wash away their sins each year during *Makar Sankranti* in January.

The major river named after *Brahma* is the Brahmaputra. In Sanskrit, Brahmaputra means "Son of Lord Brahma". Therefore amongst most rivers in the Indian subcontinent which have female names, this river has a rare male name. Brahmaputra is also one of the longest rivers in India. The Brahmaputra's upper course was long unknown, and its identity with the *Yarlung Tsangpo* in Tibet and *Siang* in Arunachal Pradesh was only established by British led explorations in 1884-86. Before this discovery, in the plains of Assam for ages the *Lohit* river was mistaken as the Brahmaputra. There are still many songs and references referring to the Brahmaputra as *Lohit* in Assam.

Since for ages in Assam, the *Lohit* river was mistaken as the Brahmaputra, is there a possibility that *Brahmakund* could have been mistakenly situated on the banks of the *Lohit* river? It appears that both elements have been named after *Lord Brahma*. If this curious case of mistaken identity is analysed logically, *Brahmakund* should be situated on the banks of the Brahmaputra. The Brahmaputra is called as the Siang in Arunachal Pradesh. Therefore there may be a remote possibility that *Brahmakund* or *Parshuram Kund* could by situated somewhere on the banks of the Siang river nearby Pasighat!

It appears that as far as Brahmaputra river and *Brahmakund* are concerned, for ages history and geography were mixed up and some rivers and places may have been wrongly sited or named. A detailed study of research works and history books may be required to resolve this perplexing confusion of names and places. If not resolved, many devotees maybe taking a dip to wash away their sins at the wrong place and wrong river! Amen!

LEGEND OF ITA FORT

One of the most romantic stories is based on Ita Fort located within the heart of Itanagar, the capital of Arunachal Pradesh. This story is based on various writings by LN Chakravarty (Glimpses of Early History of Arunachal) and Sir Edward Gait.

In ancient times there was a refugee King from Assam named *Mayamatta* who built a fort on Hita. *Mayamatta* had a beautiful queen. On becoming pregnant, due to some reason, the queen went down to the plains to give birth. The queen gave birth to a son named *Arimatta* on the banks of the Brahmaputra. The queen brought up the prince and sometime during the childhood told the prince not to venture to the north as his ancestors lived there.

After many years, *Prince Arimatta* grew up to be a great king and ruled over the area. He defeated all the kings located in the area and expanded his kingdom. On hearing that there was a King living to the north, *Arimatta* decided to march to the north to defeat the King. He gathered his troops and marched upstream along the *Dikrong* river. From there, *Arimatta* marched upstream along *Papupani* to the junction of the *Taja* and *Lepper* streams. Finally he reached place called *Ita Hills* and saw many people on the *Ita hill*, but could not advance as the door of the fort was closed.

Arimatta returned to the plains, collected more troops and re-attacked *Ita Fort*. After a tough battle, his troops managed to break the fort door and captured the fort. *Arimatta* attacked the king and tried to kill him with arrows. At this stage, the refugee king told *Arimatta* "Thou shalt not be able to kill me unless thou pierce my heart with thy fingers". *Arimatta* pierced *Mayamatta's* heart as advised, and his whole body was smeared with blood from the pierced heart. Before dying, the refugee king told *Arimatta* that he was his father!

On hearing this, *Arimatta* was filled with grief and sorrow. Then he recalled his mother's advice not to venture north. To repent for his act of patricide, *Arimatta* gave away many presents and hid many jewels, gold/silver articles in the *Goruchuntia* hills. The hidden articles are still supposed to be lying there and many people consider the place as haunted.

After returning to the plains, *Arimatta* tried to wash away his father's blood from his body by bathing in the Brahmaputra, but the stains could not be removed fully. He was full of repentance of killing his own father. Unable to withstand the remorse and guilt, on his mother's advice, *Arimatta* covered his body with oil and burnt himself to ashes.

Thus goes the legend of Ita Fort located in our Capital City!

LEGEND OF STILWELL ROAD AND THE HUMP OPERATIONS

The Stilwell Road was built during World War II by the allied forces connecting Ledo in Assam to Kunming in China. The road is named after American General Joseph Stilwell. The road is also called Ledo road. The road passes through Lekhapani, Jairampur, Nampong and Pangsau Pass of Arunachal before entering Myanmar and ending at Kunming in China. The road is 1726 km long.

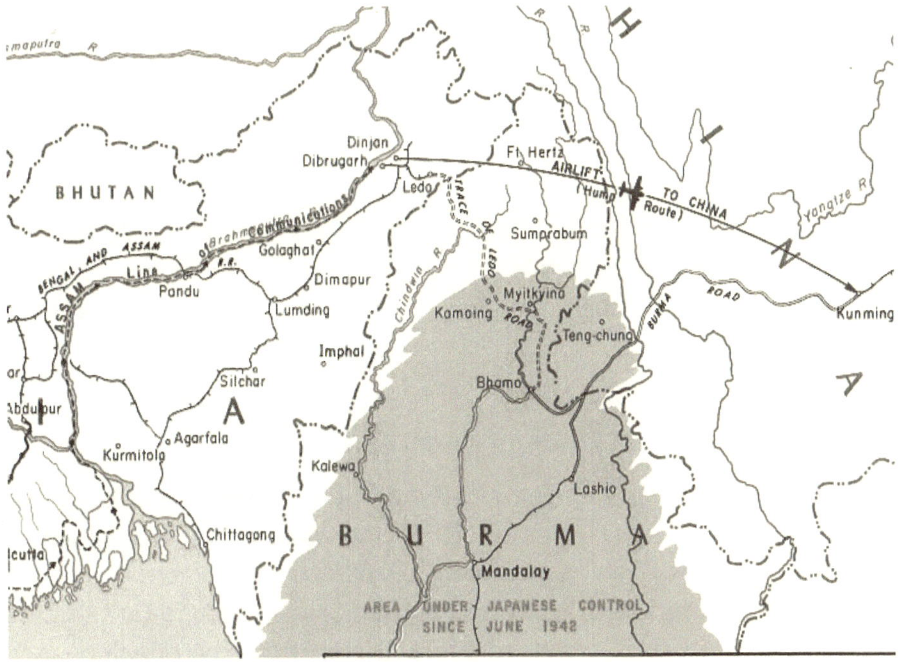

During World War II, the Allied forces supported the Chinese forces under Chiang Kai Shek against the Japanese forces. These forces were supported with weapons and supplies by transport aircraft of the allied forces. These aircraft carried supplies and weapons and flew thousands of sorties from airfields in Upper Assam to Kunming in China. These operations were called as the Hump Operations. The first over the Hump flight was flown on 08 April 1942. During the Hump Operations, 650,000 tons of materiel and supplies were airlifted to China at great cost of men and aircraft during its 42-month history. During the Hump Operations, it is estimated that the allied forces lost 594 aircraft killing 1314 airmen and passengers. In addition, 81 more aircraft were never accounted for, with 345 personnel listed as missing. Some remnants of crashed aircraft are still being discovered in remote corners of Arunachal Pradesh. Many undetonated bombs are also occasionally found from remote areas. The Hump Operations are the second biggest airlift operations in history after the Berlin Airlift operations.

The Stilwell Road was planned to augment the Hump Operations in support of Chinese forces under Chiang Kai Shek. Construction began on 16 December 1942 from Ledo. The first allied convoy reached Kunming on 04 February 1945. The allied engineers achieved the herculean task of completing the 1726 km Ledo to Kunming in about just about 2 years 1 month. The construction was amongst some of the most rough and challenging terrain and weather conditions. Many workers described the road as 'Hells Road'. The road was built by 15,000 American soldiers and 35,000 local workers at an estimated cost of US dollars 150 million. 1,100 Americans died during the construction, as well as many more locals. It is known that many Arunachali villagers participated in the construction of the road. Many Arunachali villagers lost their lives during the process of building the road.

After World War II, the Stilwell road went into disuse and the condition deteriorated because of disuse for almost sixty plus years.

Towards ushering in regional cooperation, the Stilwell or Ledo Road was recently reopened on 30 December 2015. One Chinese truck, accompanied by two light motor vehicles, carrying 82 parcels with electronic goods, organic tea, coffee, toys crossed the Pangsau Pass enroute to Guwahati to take part in the Assam International Agri-Horti Show. The opening up of the Stilwell Road may open up new avenues for Trade and Commerce in addition to building up people to people contact in the region. The opening of the road will give access to the commercially potent ASEAN markets under the Act East Policy.

8

EVOLUTION OF SOCIETY

INVERSE LAW OF EDUCATION

Most old timers will agree that many things today are quite different and opposite to what things were few decades back.

There was a time when 'Bell-Bottom' trousers, big collars, high heeled shoes and long hair were stylish. Today trendy men's fashion includes short trouser bottoms, small collars, flat shoes and short hair. Earlier we worked by day and slept by night...now many of us sleep till late in the day and stay awake deep into the night. Earlier we had more children and no maids... today we have lesser children and more maids! Earlier there were no TVs, computers and mobiles, so people spent more time with family, friends and played outdoor games in extra time...today each member is so busy with TV, computer and mobile that there is no time left to spend with your loved ones and play outdoor games. Earlier petty thieves caught in villages stealing fowl, domesticated animals or rare ornaments were out casted from the village...today persons plundering public money and property are called as Chief Guests, Guests of Honour and garlanded!!

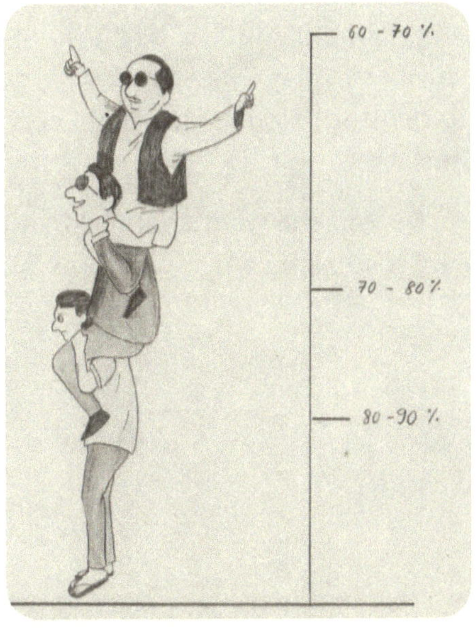

Similarly, many observers feel that there is an inverse logic in the field of education vis-a-vis power. The most brilliant in studies at school clear the competitive examinations after Class XII and become Engineers, Doctors, Army/Navy/Airforce officers. Those who could not make it to engineering, medicine and armed forces opt for graduation in other fields like arts, science, commerce, law etc. Immediately after graduation they again clear other competitive exams and join Central Police forces, PSUs, MNCs etc. Amongst students left out many attempt Civil Services Exams and become central services officers like IAS, IPS, IRS etc. Those who could not qualify for all these professions become politicians. And many who do not complete their studies become DONs!

A minor analysis would reveal the hierarchy of power. The DON dictates the Politicians; the Politicians dictate the Bureaucrats; the Bureaucrats dictate the Central Police Services, PSUs, Armed Forces, Engineers, Doctors etc! In this inverse logic, the most brilliant students end up at the bottom of the job pyramid and the average students reach the top of the job pyramid!

While this may be a generic observation and may not apply to all cases, it is an indication that just being brilliant in studies is not a guarantee to get the best job or post. A study of profile of many successful persons will reveal that the formula of becoming successful in life includes a combination of being good in studies, being good in other co-curricular, extracurricular activities, being smart and some good guidance by parents/relatives. A quick glance around you might confirm the validity of this Inverse Law of Education.

Do you still want your children to be brilliant in studies? Do you still want to run after arduous tuitions and chase dreams of IITs and IIMs?

Unlearning the Learnt

Most successful Arunachalese have studied outside the state at some stage of their student life. Since there were no medical, engineering and law colleges in the state, almost all engineers, doctors and lawyers have attended college outside the state. Because of availability of only few colleges, many Arunachalese studied in colleges outside the state.

Today, many forward looking students who have performed well in Class XII exams and children from affluent families undertake graduate and post graduate studies in Delhi, Chennai, Bengaluru, Mumbai, Pune, Kolkata, Dehradun etc. For school education also many students are opting to studies outside the state. Many students are pursuing school education in prominent residential schools at places like Guwahati, Tezpur, Numaligarh, Delhi, Dehradoon, Bengaluru, Shillong etc.

Arunachalese educated outside the state interact and mingle with other students of different cultures, castes, tribes, races and regions. Studying in major metropolitan cities, they are exposed to pillars of development like expressways, swanky shopping malls, flyovers, metro rails, modern airports, elite universities, multiplexes, museums, planetariums etc. They are taught by accomplished professors, lecturers and taken on exposure visits to famous institutions. They are exposed to lofty concepts like idealism, fraternity, pluralism, secularism, socialism, democracy etc.

Similarly many Arunachali officers attend seminars and conferences in swanky convention centres in major cities of India and few lucky ones attend such seminars in foreign countries. In these seminars and conferences, they are exposed to latest developments in education, superior economic theories, latest development concepts, management formulas etc where they mingle and interact with the best minds of the nation and the world.

After such exposure and grooming for many years in various colleges and universities of the world in the prime, influential years of their lives, most Arunachalese return home bubbling with new ideas and zeal to implement new concepts in their home state. However, their enthusiasm and zeal is muzzled after a few years in the state. Soon these lofty concepts and theories are compromised by the lifestyle prevalent in the land of *Khushi Khushi*. Most concepts learnt in the institutions outside the state are gradually forgotten and dumped into the dustbins to be replaced by omnipresent local lethargy and inertia. Such is the lethargy and inertia that, many modern development concepts are reversed, and regressive concepts are implemented with gusto and vigour!

This reversal of modern ideas and concepts have been the bane of our state due to which our state remains one of the lesser developed states of the country. If majority of the concepts learned outside the state were sustained and implemented, maybe Arunachal would have been propelled towards the path of development. May be all these ideas need an enabling environment? Can we provide that? Or perhaps, we need stronger character to retain, sustain and implement modern concepts leaned outside the state!

LOSING OUR YOUTH

"The child is the father of the man" ... *"Children are the future of the world"* are commonly used quotes. The population of youth is multiplying by manifolds in India. About half of India's 133 Crores population is under the age of 25. About two-thirds are less than 35 years. By 2020, the average age in India will be 29 years and it is set to become the world's youngest country. It implies that the future of our nation and the world depends primarily on the youth.

With this burgeoning young population, the nation and the world face the daunting task of providing suitable employment opportunities to these restless youth. Lack of job opportunities is leading to frustration in many youth and many disgruntled youth are resorting to other harmful distractions like drugs, alcohol, smoking etc.

The other aspect dampening the prospects of youth is the lure for harmful habits like smoking, drinking and drug addiction. Being groomed by tribal lifestyle many youth get exposed to drinking alcohol at a very young age. Many youth start emulating the adults by drinking alcohol even during day. The odd aspect typical to North East India is that women also drink almost at par with men! Similarly many adults are addicted to drugs like Opium and *bhang* in our villages. Therefore children are exposed to drugs at an early age.

Other aspects shortening the lives of our youth is drunken driving, underage driving and drowning in rivers and lakes. A common sight in our state is the prevalence of many Scooties/Bikes parked outside our high/higher secondary schools. It is a common feature to see young school boys and girls openly driving Scooties/Bikes in school uniform! These errant students are not checked by teachers, school staff, police etc. In fact many parents encourage their underage children to drive to school!

In most tourist spots, riversides, lakesides one of the most distasteful sights is that of littered beer cans and liquor bottles. There is a report that Arunachal has the highest per capita IMFL consumption in the nation! Many youth have been lost due to drunken driving and drowning caused by entering the rivers/lakes in a drunken state.

Due to dependencies on expensive liquor, smoking, drugs etc many youth are resorting to lying to parents or blackmailing parents. Some youth are resorting to theft, arson and loot to meet their expensive tastes. Once addicted to these vices, many students start missing classes and dropping out of schools all together.

Many youth have talent. As a society, maybe we are failing to provide a healthy platform for our youth to perform and excel. There are very few Govt schemes and NGOs venturing into this sensitive but important aspect of grooming our youth. Even the many student/youth bodies are busy with bigger issues of governance rather than grooming our misguided youth. Misguided youth needs to be groomed and brought back into the mainstream of our society. Else our future is bleak. It is a Clear and present danger!

How Bad Is Being Good...?

"All that is necessary for evil to prevail is for good people to do nothing."

It is traditionally considered that the 'Good People' are well educated in good schools and colleges and are groomed to be humble, polite, well mannered, civil etc. They are taught to dress formally, stand in queues and wait for their chances to speak. These pedigreed persons dress well, talk quietly, politely and avoid shouting matches. They tend to avoid highly congested areas and ghettoes unless unavoidable.

On the other hand, the 'Bad People' are brusque, aggressive and are go-getters. They do not hesitate to engage in shouting duels and likes to dominate situations and persons. Some of them are less educated and exposed to petty crimes, violent acts at an early age which trains them to absorb body blows.

In life, it is often seen that the miniscule 'Bad Persons' dominate, manipulate and exploit the majority 'Good Persons'.

In a crowded movie hall, a bunch of few rowdies will make life miserable for remaining hundreds of movie watchers. The majority will keep quiet for fear of violence and accept spoiling the movie show. Similar is the case with small time extortionists who extort money in small groups. The majority will quietly give money for fear of violence and to avoid trouble.

Very often, it is seen that *bandhs* are enforced by small groups of 10-15 people. These small groups create chaos amongst the entire population of the area. Even the police and security forces remain mute spectators.

Recent media coverage in many cities shows how the majority public remain mute bystanders as women were being molested by few goons. Similar footages of public apathy are frequently seen wherein serious accident/medical victims are ignored by majority of vehicles and pedestrians.

Something similar occurs in governments, politics and societies. Small groups of persons create policies, rules and regulations to abet pilferage of public money, assets and property. They create 'Exclusive Ghettoes' of elite persons to jointly plunder public money, assets and property. The majority public consisting of senior citizens, farmers, villagers, Govt employees, businessmen, traders etc keep quiet and suffer silently.

It is a known fact that many well educated and elite persons do not vote. The voting class are majorly the middle and lower class. As a result, many governments are elected by middle and lower classes votes. The well educated elite must take responsibility for getting the kind of governments we are getting!!

Good persons do not fight...good persons do not argue...good persons do not shout...good persons do not protest...good persons do not intervene... good persons do not vote...!!! Generally good persons are apathetic and indifferent. They do their own duties well and leave problems of society to the others!!

Is it fair to conclude that the 10 % 'Bad' dictate, manipulate and exploit the 90 % 'Good'?

Is it acceptable for good persons to remain 'Good' and do nothing? Basically majority of the people are 'Good at Heart'...it is just that the 'Goodness' has to bloom from the binding force of 'Badness'! History shows that when the majority 'Good People' awaken, revolutions occur. Are we waiting for a revolution?

IS BEING GOOD BAD...?

BLAME IT ON RIO...!

As 'Healthy able bodied' human beings, we consider ourselves infallible. On most occasions, we blame others for any mistakes. We brand mistake makers in the *Second Person* like 'It was your fault....', 'The error was because of you....' or *Third Person* like 'His mistake..., Her fault..., They messed it up...'. That means mistakes not by me or us; but by You, Him, Her or Them.... In other words, in case of a mistake/error, blame somebody else!

This state of denial further leads to blaming everybody or everything else except own self. In case the laid down objectives were not achieved, ready excuses like the delay was due to so many *bandhs*...the vehicle broke down...I was not feeling well...are resorted to cover up own shortcomings. Generally the instant we make mistakes the instinctive response is to look for suitable alibis! If we wake up late and can't make it to office on time, we instantly look for excuses......What should be my excuse...? The bike did not start...I had a tyre puncture...I will sneak in from the side door...there was too much traffic and so on!

The reverse logic applies in case of good deeds and major achievements. Since we consider ourselves error free, we lay sole claim to good things/ achievements! The general instinctive reaction to any event is to claim all good results and blame all bad results on somebody/something else. If the election was won, it was because of me. If the election was lost it was because of the party...supporters...volunteers...not me! Similarly in case of a good show, 'It was my idea'! If the plan does not work as planned.....the party did not help out....there were no resources.....it was just bad luck...!

The Government is bad...politicians are bad...government officers are bad...engineers are bad...contractors are bad...BUT...I/we are good...!! For schools, we teachers are good...students are bad...! Arunachalese are good...*harings* are bad...! Our tribe is good...other tribes are bad...! Our generation was good...the next generation/our children have no values...! The blame game carries on.

Since some of us exist in a state wherein we blame somebody else for most of our shortcomings, we are not ready to identify and accept our own mistakes or weaknesses. This further leads to expecting 'second and third persons' to solve the existing problems while insulating own selves. This holier than thou attitude leads to the prolonged existence of identifiable and solvable weaknesses in us or in society. If we are able to relate inherent own weaknesses in all associated incidents/problems, we will initiate necessary corrective actions which will further lead to a healthy and efficient environment.

A deeper soul searching/analysis may reveal that many faults blamed on somebody else/others actually originate from us. The first step may be is to stop 'Blaming it on Rio' or somebody else for our problems and understand that 'It may be our/my fault'! As a start, should we look deeper within ourselves before blaming others?

Rules Are for Others...not for Me...!

'ONE PERSON AT A TIME' is written outside most ATMs in big letters...

'PLEASE CARRY MOBILES IN SILENT MODE' is written outside most banks...

'NO MOBILES PLEASE' is written at all Petrol Pumps...

'NO MOBILES WHILE DRIVING' is a rule told to all...

'PLEASE DON'T SPIT HERE' is written on many walls...

As per Merriam Webster, *Rule* is defined as 'a prescribed guide for conduct or action…a statement that tells you what is allowed or what will happen within a particular system…an accepted procedure, custom, or habit…'

It you are one of the lucky ones to visit an ATM, the typical scene is very interesting. The queue at the ATM starts from the ATM machine inside the ATM booth. In fact the person standing behind you is trying to push you inside the machine itself! The person is leaning over you and prompting you to push the right push buttons! So much for confidentiality of ATM codes!

At traffic crossings, red, amber and green lights are fitted to regulate traffic to avoid accidents which may result in loss of precious lives. Some of us however feel that these lights are meant for others…therefore jump red/amber lights. We may get away once in a while…but the clock is ticking towards a waiting collision and an accident.

Mobiles are not meant to be used at Petrol Pumps due to the danger of creating an explosion by the electric charge in mobiles. This is for our own safety. However we regularly witness people routinely speaking on mobiles at Petrol Pumps.

Using mobile while driving is an offence. Many accidents have been caused by drivers whose attention has been diverted due to mobile usage while driving. However we regularly see drivers talking or texting on the mobile while driving. In fact many times we see people speaking on mobiles while driving two wheelers! Many lives have been lost due to mobile usage while driving.

We all have gone through the frustration of waiting for persons to arrive for a meeting/appointment. We don't like waiting and curse people who make us wait. Do you also arrive late for a meeting/appointment or office and make other people wait? Being on time is not only for others…it applies to us also!

How many times have you seen VIPs and high ranking officials parking their vehicle exactly where NO PARKING is written? Have you ever entered a NO ENTRY road? Have you seen people spitting inside ATMs, offices, shops etc?

In most advanced societies or countries, people obey rules without questioning them. They are groomed from childhood by parents, teachers and leaders with personal examples. This is because they realize that rules are put in place for the good of society. They realize that rules are applicable to everyone including self, however senior he or she might be!

DO YOU STILL CONSIDER YOURSELF OUTSIDE RULES?

Urban Migration

Urban Migration is a global phenomenon altering the demographic map of many countries. Urbanisation is taking place at a rapid rate in India, North East & Arunachal also. Urban population has increased from 11 % in 1901 to 32 % in 2011 census. Every minute, 25-30 people are migrating to Indian cities from rural areas!

North East and Arunachal are witnessing similar increased migration by young villagers to Capital region, District HQs and major towns. In fact many villages near major towns are left with mostly elderly population who are sticking to the villages due legacy and tradition while most young persons have already migrated to towns! Many villages are not finding sufficient students for schools in the villages. Very few youth are taking up the traditional profession of their forefathers like farming or agri-horticulture. In fact most villagers are today dependent on migrant labourers.

People are migrating to cities in search of better economic benefits, better education, better medical facilities & more jobs. This urban migration is overwhelming the few towns and cities. Many towns are witnessing unplanned growth with lack of water supply, electricity, drainage, parking space, children parks, playgrounds etc. This is further leading to increase in pollution, traffic jams, crime, drug addiction, alcoholism etc. Unless this fast paced urban migration is stemmed, our towns and cities are headed for chaos and collapse.

There are no easy solutions to this complex problem of urban migration. Every person wants to taste town life, better education, health care, shopping malls, multiplexes etc. Govt, intellectuals, elders and society must step in with some innovative methods to slow this urban migration.

One way to stem urban migration is by improving rural infrastructure like stable electricity, water supply, mobile/internet connectivity and good roads between towns and villages. If there are good roads, stable electricity, mobile/internet connectivity, good schools in rural areas lesser people are likely to migrate from villages. Other way could be to strengthen the Panchayati Raj system wherein financial and executive power is vested with Panchayati Raj institutions of rural areas. Another option could be to shift main offices of State Govt and District HQs to nearby rural areas away from cities. For example the Capital of Gujarat is at Gandhinagar which is in a rural area 30-35 km away from the city of Ahmedabad. Another example is Yupia, the District HQ of Papumpare. One option could be to shift major industries, educational institutes/universities, central institutes to rural areas. This would create more job opportunities in rural areas and uplift the rural economy. Another way maybe is by making rural livelihood options like agri-horticulture, livestock rearing, fisheries etc more attractive with incentives, grants, assured markets, subsidies etc.

Urban migration is killing our towns & cities which are over-populated, polluted, dirty and chaotic. As responsible citizens we must all must contribute to stem this menace of urban migration. Do you still want to live in cities & towns?

Peace Index...!

As per the latest Global Peace Index (GPI) rankings, India is ranked very low at 141 among 163 countries. Every year GPI measures the relative position of nations' and regions' peacefulness. Towards assessing peacefulness, GPI studies the extent to which countries are involved in internal and external conflicts. It also analyses the level of harmony or discord within a nation; ten indicators broadly assess what might be described as safety and security in society. The contention is that low crime rates, minimal incidences of terrorist acts, violent demonstrations, harmonious relations with neighboring countries, a stable political scene and a small proportion of the population being internally displaced or refugees can be suggestive of peacefulness. The parameters considered for these rankings includes factors like Number/ duration of internal conflicts, Impact of terrorism, Political instability, Number of internal security officers/ police per 100,000 people, Number of homicides, Level of violent crime, Number of refugees/ displaced persons as percentage of population etc.

Ironically factors like Gross Domestic Product, Economic soundness are not considered for peace index. Factors considered are related to tolerance for other religions, tolerance for other races/ castes, other customs/ traditions, for other's eating habits, dressing habits etc.

As per the present GPI rankings Iceland remains the most peaceful nation and Afghanistan the least peaceful nation. However it is revealed that India's ranking is below Bhutan (15 Rank), Sri Lanka (72), Nepal (76), Bangladesh (101), China (110), Myanmar (125). In the Sub Continent only Pakistan and Afghanistan are below India!

Major religions that preach peaceful co-existence and tolerance like Budhism, Jainism, Hinduism, Sikhism etc have originated in India. In fact the father of the nation is Mahatma Gandhi who preached Ahimsa or non-violence. Many believe that Mahatma Gandhi's Ahimsa or non-violent movement finally led to India attaining freedom from British rule. Despite all these peaceful milestones why is our great nation ranked so low in the peace index?

Internally we have ongoing violent conflicts in many states of central India, Jammu & Kashmir and all states of North East India. Externally we have fought wars in 1948, 1962, 1965, 1971. There were armed interventions in Sri Lanka, Maldives and armed conflicts like Kargil operations, Operation Parakram, Mumbai terror attacks etc.

Are we quarrelsome and intolerant? Are we short-tempered and aggressive? Are our lives dominated by tension and anxiety? Are our lives dominated by protests, conflicts and violence that our country is rated so low in the peace index?

Most of our news headlines on TV, print media, social media are dominated by violent news, protests, religious/racial conflicts, political slugfests. Today's news channels are like boxing matches with all participants and anchors shouting over each other.

Are we peaceful and happy in North East India and Arunachal? Isn't it time that India, North East and Arunachal strive towards more peace and stability in society? We owe it to our next generations!

Life Teachers

A few days back on 05 September, Teachers Day was celebrated across the nation. Teachers Day is celebrated in honour of *Bharat Ratna* Dr Sarvapalli Radhakrishnan who was India's second President and a scholar/philosopher. In Arunachal Pradesh, Teacher's Day was also celebrated throughout the state with cultural functions and programmes in different schools and colleges.

Teachers have a major impact on our lives. Most people may not remember people like the richest person of the world, most powerful person of the world etc. However, most people will remember their teachers by name, especially the teachers of primary and middle schools. In many cases, teachers are the first role models for children. Being at an impressionable age, many young children look up to their teachers and want to emulate them in character, etiquette and behaviour.

After parents, Teachers have the onerous task of educating and grooming our children from a very young age. Many teachers perform this important role under demanding circumstances. Teacher's salaries are low, many schools do not have basic amenities like electricity, water, toilets etc, there is lack of quarters and in many cases some teachers are not paid salaries for months. In few remote corners of our state, teachers have to walk for few days to reach the schools in the villages.

However, are teachers the only profession to take on this onerous responsibility of educating and grooming our next generations? Can Parents, Elders and society shy away from this responsibility? Most schools provide just academic education to our children. Many parents expect that once children are in school, it is the teacher's responsibility to educate and groom them. The responsibility of teaching and grooming our children to transform them into responsible citizens of the nation must be shared by parents, elders and society.

Most teachers teach the children to be honest, disciplined and sincere. Children are taught these important values by teachers. But many children pick up bad traits like cheating, cunningness, arrogance etc from parents, relatives and society. In olden days, to groom our children well there was a book on Moral Values. Today it is assumed that most students are honest, possess good character and thus the formal lessons on moral values have been removed from the syllabi in many schools!

The profession of teaching is so noble and attractive that many successful professionals opt for teaching post retirement. The former President of India, APJ Abdul Kalam went back to teaching after retiring! Other such teachers include Rabindranath Tagore and Albert Einstein.

The other baffling aspect is the performance of government schools vis-á-vis private schools. Though government schools are well funded and teachers paid relatively well, results show that private schools with poorly paid teachers are performing better. Another modern day puzzle!!

Strategic Thought...!

Arunachal Pradesh is the only state in India to share borders with three countries. Arunachal shares 160 km border with Bhutan, 440 km with Myanmar and 1030 km with China. Being a border state, strategic planning for all major infrastructure projects in the state is a necessity.

In North West India, the 660 km long Indira Gandhi canal running through the states of Punjab, Haryana and Rajasthan is a major obstacle for enemy tanks and armoured vehicles. In case of an enemy attack by armoured vehicles, the enemy would be forced to stop at the canal.

The capital of Russia, Moscow has 12 Levels of underground metro. The metro not only expedited travelling within the city; it was also a huge nuclear shelter. In case of any nuclear attack, the best shelter is underground. Similarly, metros built underground in Delhi, Kolkata, Bengaluru etc can also double up as nuclear shelters.

During the cold war in the USA, no building plans were cleared without an underground shelter/cellar. These shelters/cellars were stocked with food and essential items to cater for nuclear fall outs.

Roads and railways built in Border States are also strategically planned catering for deployment of defence personnel and equipment. In earlier days railway lines existed at major army/ air force bases to allow rapid movement of ammunition and weaponry. Even construction of critical bridges across major rivers like Brahmaputra, Subansiri, Kameng, Siang, Lohit has to cater for rapid deployment of defence personnel and equipment.

All weather roads will allow rapid deployment of heavy equipment like artillery guns and armoured vehicles at forward locations. Since major railway networks are not possible in mountainous areas, all weather roads up to border posts are a must for robust defence of the state and nation.

Critical bridges over major rivers like Brahmaputra, Siang, Subansiri, Lohit, Kameng etc are also key targets for the enemy. These bridges must be painted in camouflage colours to prevent easy detection from the air. This will increase the difficulty level to target these bridges with missiles. Camouflage and concealment is a professional subject and wide choice of visual camouflage, Infra Red camouflage, paints etc are available. These critical bridges also need to be defended by surface to air missiles and ground forces.

Since the few bridges across the Brahmaputra can be easily targeted, strategic planning dictates that a few Oil Depots, Ammunition Dumps etc should be constructed on the northern bank of the Brahmaputra to support military operations in Arunachal Pradesh.

Civil airports can be easily used by defence aircraft. Construction of civil airports at strategic location will allow rapid deployment of personnel and equipment.

One of the prime targets of the enemy would be command and control centres. Therefore national and state leadership may also be prime targets. Therefore, the Central Secretariats and Head offices should also be painted in camouflage colours to merge with the background. Presently these buildings are painted and decorated with bright colours!

For robust defence of the state and nation, strategic planning in all infrastructure projects is a necessity.

Isn't it better to Sweat in Peace than to Bleed in War?

Harder Right or Easier Wrong!

Harder Right over Easier Wrong...!! Is this an oxymoron...a combination of contradictory words like *deafening silence...natural actor...true story..?* Or...is this a universally true statement..?

Are right things always hard..? Are easier things always wrong..?

At our alma mater National Defence Academy, our every day prayer went like this. 'O Lord...help us to choose the Harder Right over the Easier Wrong....'

Ask any good student and he will tell you that to get good grades at the board examinations, students have to slog hard...study day and night. Along with the students, parents and teachers have to work equally hard to guide the students in getting good grades.

However, the easier way for some students/parents could be to relax the whole year...copy in the exams to get good grades. Another easy way could be to get a leaked question paper before the exams or rig the evaluators/officials to achieve good results!

In today's competitive world, clearing the series of examinations/interviews for qualifying competitive examinations like Civil Services, APSC etc would entail years of preparation, undergoing tough & expensive tuition courses and maybe many attempts at the examinations.

However, the easier way could be to use a Minister's recommendations or pay some 'management fees' to the right people to qualify easily (...remember Madhya Pradesh's VYAPAM Scam)!

Any farmer, businessmen, entrepreneur will testify with own experience that doing well and making money honestly involves lot of hard work, sacrifice and years of dedication. Even after years of hard work and toil only a lucky few have become rich and successful.

Similarly, any successful athlete will vouch that it requires years of training, discipline and sweat to get a podium position. Unless of course the athlete resorts to the easier method of boosting his performance by using steroids or stimulant drugs.

Even in government service, everyone is in a queue and has to put in many years of dedicated service to reach the top post.

In real life, there are no escalators to success...only steps...to be climbed one by one!!

If anyone becomes rich overnight, it is likely that he or she has pilfered somebody else's money. On very rare occasions, few very lucky persons gets rich by winning a lottery...However, it appears that in this world many people have frequently won million dollar lotteries that also many times in their careers..!!

Choosing the harder right involves steely resolve and high integrity. In the long run achieving success through honest means, without taking shortcuts and cheating, the satisfaction and recognition is unmatched.

Historically, every society or nation that has done well have nurtured these fundamental values like honesty, integrity, discipline, hard work etc. Almost all these societies have chosen the harder right over the easier wrong!

DO WE ALSO WANT TO CHOOSE THE HARDER RIGHT?

EDUCATION AND WISDOM

*"Wisdom is not a product of Schooling But of the
lifelong attempt to acquire it."*

- Albert Einstein

As per Wikipedia, Wisdom is the ability to think and act using knowledge, experience, understanding, common sense and insight. Wisdom has been regarded as one of four cardinal virtues; and as a virtue.

All parents desire that their children get the best education this world has on offer. They want their children to study languages, math, science, history, social studies etc during school and college. Parents expect that good education in school and a good result would lead to a placement in a reputed college. Education in a good school and college would further lead to the child getting a well paid job in the Government or in a reputed company. A good job will make the child independent, enhance the reputation of the family and maybe fetch a good bride/groom!

However, schools and colleges concentrate mainly on academic (scholastic) education. For grooming of children, schools and colleges include some co-curricular and extra-curricular activities in the curriculum. However, subjects like moral education, good behaviour, humility... leadership qualities like honesty, integrity are not taught to the students in organised classes. Very less emphasis is paid to teaching the children about their rights, duties and responsibilities. Mostly grooming of children in these virtues are left to the immediate family, relatives and society as a large.

Education arms a child with theoretical knowledge without major emphasis on character building qualities. A child's upbringing is said to be good when they are humble, obedient, polite and courteous. If the child does okay in academics, co-curricular and extra-curricular activities, it is an added bonus. It is generally expected that children who have attended reputed school and college, placed at a first class job and whose upbringing has been good generally grow up into wise men.

However we have seen many of our Gaon Buras and village elders possessing wisdom despite being less educated and less travelled. On the other side, we also have met highly educated people who have travelled extensively, being absolutely worldly wise with minimal moral ethics. Many of these officers are educated in professional colleges outside the state. Despite being well educated and well exposed to all facets of life, many of them indulge in unfair practices, display arrogance of money, position and care a hoot about moral ethics. In fact, it may not be wrong to state that some of them possess much lesser wisdom than many uneducated villagers!

Today's children are smarter than the older generation. It is not an easy task to groom/counsel them to be wise men or women. To groom them, parents, elders, teachers have to demonstrate integrity, honesty and moral character of a high order with personal examples. Honesty, integrity, discipline, humility, good manners etc are the founding stones for grooming a child into a mature and responsible citizen. Citizens of most advanced nations possess these fundamental values of integrity, honesty, discipline, humility, helpfulness etc of a high order.

Many of us have seen that most tribal villagers possessed these fundamental qualities of integrity, honesty, humility, helpfulness etc of a high order. The pertinent question therefore is...WHERE HAVE THESE VALUES VANISHED? Have good education and modernisation made us less wise?

ROLE MODELS FOR SOCIETY!

In society, Role Models play a very important role in deciding the future of our children. Good Role Models will inspire children to inculcate right values which would further lead to a healthier and robust society.

The earliest role models for children are parents and teachers. Parents and teachers play a very important role in the initial grooming of children leading to children wanting to emulate them. If parents and teachers teach or exhibit good qualities and values, children get positively inspired at a young age.

Movies and media also play an important role in selection of role models. Many children aim to become pilots after watching movies like *'Top Gun'* and *'Aradhana'*. Many want to become Soldiers after watching war movies like *'Border'* and *'Behind Enemy Lines'*.

Children are impressed by many things. Big cars, big houses, lots of property impress children. Easy life, high flying lifestyle are big motivators. Rich people are powerful; money moves things and influences decisions.

As they grow up, children observe and learn. When they observe many people amassing disproportionate wealth, property and find them getting away, they realise that they can also become such a person without major risks. They decide to emulate them.

As per McGregor's Management Theory X, human beings are basically lazy and do not want to work. If one can achieve name and fame without working hard, then why work and waste energy!! Learning from society, many children start changing their childhood aims in their teenage years.

Today, very few children want to be farmers, scientists, mathematicians, research scholars, pilots, soldiers or entrepreneurs. Since children observe many people becoming rich and powerful without being exposed to major risks to their careers and lives, they end up choosing such professions with easy access to public money.

On a flip side, can becoming a 'Thug or Thief' be an aim in life? Do any children want to become a *Dawood Ibrahim or Phoolan Devi*? Do parents or teachers want their children to become mafia bosses or Dons? After all getting punished and jailed at the twilight of life would not be the aim of life!!

Many modern and civilised nations imbibe and practice strong traits like honesty, integrity, discipline, sincerity etc. These successful societies have many strong Role Models and leaders exhibiting these strong values. In these societies, these strong values are exhibited by many political leaders also!

Does our society have the right Role Models?

Generation Change...!

There is a saying that there is a 'Generation Change' in every 25-30 years. This 'Generation Change' is accompanied by changes in technology, dress, personal styles and habits. These generation changes vary from gradual to drastic.

There was a time when 'Bell-Bottom' trousers and high heeled shoes were stylish for men...now there are no 'Bell-Bottoms' to be seen. In olden days, women wore maxi-skirts...today women wear hot pants. Big shirt collars were stylish once upon of time...today many shirts do not even have collars! Earlier there was only one soap called *Lifebouy*...it was used commonly for body, hair and face by both males and females...now there are different types of facewash, body shower gels, hand creams, foot creams and shampoo-conditioners for hair!

Earlier we lived in elongated *kutcha* houses without rooms...now we have RCC houses with many rooms...one room for each member...! Earlier families live as joint families. Now each son and daughter has separate houses. Earlier our houses were kept unlocked because there was nothing worthwhile to be stolen...today our houses have big walls, multiple locks, grills and lockers to stash our money and ornaments.

Earlier we worked by day and slept by night...now many of us sleep till late in the day and stay awake deep into the night. Earlier we worked hard, walked more and stayed fit...now we sit in offices for hours, drive around in vehicles and eat more!

Earlier we had more children and no maids...today we have lesser children and more maids! Earlier there were no TVs, computers and mobiles, so people spent more time with family, friends and played outdoor games in extra time...today each member is so busy with TV, Computer and mobile that there is no time left to spend with your loved ones and play outdoor games.

Earlier the few roads were empty for us to drive and walk freely...today there are so many vehicles that roads are jammed and there are no parking places!

Earlier we ate organic food...we ate local vegetables, local eggs, local fowls, local fish...today we eat eggs from Andhra and West Bengal, fish from Andhra, broiler chicken from West Bengal. Organic vegetables and meat are rare these days.

Earlier petty thieves caught in villages stealing fowl, domesticated animals or rare ornaments were out casted from the village...today persons plundering public money and property are called as Chief Guests, Guests of Honour and garlanded!!

Earlier we were less educated but more mature and wise...today we are more educated, more travelled...but intolerant, irrational, impolite, egoistic and more corrupt!!

After a generation change...'Are we better off today?'

WHY STUDY...SILLY?

Why should students study hard? Today students start studying from about 3 years of age in Play Schools and continue for the next 15 years to pass Class XII. After Class XII a student studies for another 5-11 years to get a decent job. Altogether a student has to go through the rigmarole of going to school / college / university, home works, tuitions, entrance exams, interviews for almost 20-26 years of his life! Most people are about 24-30 years of age by the time they settle down in a job.

Despite these hardships, world over, most young boys and girls study hard to achieve their aims and goals. It is a proven fact that doing well in school / college / university is the fundamental stepping stone to successful careers and lives. It is accepted that students who study well go on to having good jobs, living comfortable lives and become leaders. Students who are poor in studies end up with lower grade jobs and lead obscure careers and lives.

Most Arunachali leaders, bureaucrats, teachers, parents and society also understand the importance of a good education system and want their children to perform well. Most schools, teachers, parents try their best to enable the students to do well in their exams. Any responsible parents, teachers, leaders do not want children to fail. Then, why is the performance of our students so poor year after year? This year the pass percentage of Class X is a meagre 21 % and 44 % for Class XII.

What is wrong with our education system? Why can't our children speak and write satisfactory English? Why can't our children solve simple math, science problems and understand simple social sciences? Why can't our children pass their exams? Schools are in place...there are teachers, directors, secretaries, educationists to plan and implement school curriculum and management. Almost every person in the educational system seems to be doing their assigned jobs. If all is satisfactory, what is ailing in our education system?

Many educationists and intellectuals blame the infamous Comprehensive Continuous Evaluation (CCE) System introduced for few years by the previous Govt under which, there were negligible failures and Class X board exams were made optional. Almost everyone was guaranteed to pass and no syllabus was repeated!

However, is CCE the sole reason for poor results of students? There may be some other intangible factors which indirectly effect student psyche. Is it that our children simply are not motivated enough to study well? Are wrong Role Models being promoted by our society? As parents, leaders and as a society are we setting wrong examples? Are students learning easier ways of earning a livelihood by joining political affiliations, joining youth/student organisations, becoming contractors, housie/lottery organisers etc? Do our students feel that why study so hard for so many years when comfortable livelihood may be acquired by easier means?

Arunachali students and parents are no less than other students and parents. There is a requirement to re-prioritise and refocus our values as a society to strive for excellence in education and work hard enough. However, any ideas as to why most students of private schools seems to be performing better that Govt schools?

IS GANDHIGIRI RELEVANT TODAY?

Recently on 02 October the nation celebrated Gandhi Jayanti to honour Father of the Nation Mahatma Gandhi. Gandhi Jayanti is solemnly celebrated throughout Arunachal with functions & prayers. United Nation has also declared 02 October as International Day of Non-Violence in honour of Mahatma Gandhi.

Mahatma Gandhi led India to freedom from British rule without weapons or army through Non-Violence. Normally, non-violence is taken as weakness, but Gandhiji showed the world that non-violence & tolerance are great weapons. He said "The weak can never forgive. Forgiveness is the attribute of the strong." Other principles espoused by Gandhiji were Truth, Equality, Secularism, Swacchta etc. Gandhiji's life was the finest example of 'Simple Living High Thinking' and his followers included Nelson Mandela, Martin Luther King, Dalai Lama, Aung San Suu Kyi.

Against Gandhiji's principle of Ahimsa, violent protests & clashes are increasing in the world. Many wars are being fought over national/state boundaries, religions, caste, race, river sharing, economics etc. Hundreds of terrorist groups are operating in numerous countries. Thousands of humans are losing their lives in battles or terrorist related violence. Minor disagreements or clashes are triggering people to take up arms and attack each other.

These increasing cases of violence and intolerance is being flamed and fuelled by recent narrative of extreme right wing nationalism & opinions. Narratives like 'If you are not with us, you are against us' are being propounded. These differences are manifesting in violent clashes. Between nations, conflicts occur due disputes over territory, river sharing, religion, economics. Within nations, humans are clashing over race, caste, religion, injustice etc.

Against Gandhiji's principles of Truthfulness, many are lying habitually. Honesty & truthfulness have become rare qualities. Regarding equality also India is the second most unequal country in the world with top one per cent of the population owning nearly 60% of the wealth! Castism and racism are prevalent in many parts of the nation. Many conflicts & clashes within India are also caused by religious intolerance!

Even in our area, honesty & truthfulness are gradually decreasing. Regarding conflicts, it is estimated that there are hundreds of *Kebangs/ Mels* going on per day in our villages & towns to resolve disputes over land, property, marital disputes, theft etc! Reactions to minor disputes are typically *'Kaat or Maar Dunga'!* Racism, clanism is also increasing in our state.

Ironically, Gandhiji's principles are more relevant today. Like his quote *"An eye for eye only ends up making the whole world blind",* in the long run violence breeds more violence making us more insecure and unhappy. Similarly many civilised societies & nations who display higher degrees of honesty & truthfulness are more stable, peaceful & developed! Likewise many nations are imbibing and adopting the principles of secularism, equality etc.

Do you believe in Gandhiji's principles of Ahimsa, Honesty, Equality, Secularism and Tolerance? By the way Mahatma Gandhi was never awarded the Bharat Ratna and 02 October is also marked as Dry Day!!

Compulsory NCC for Students?

Recently a 10 Days Combined Annual Training Camp for National Cadet Corps (NCC) Cadets was conducted by 22 Arunachal Pradesh (I) Company, Pasighat in which about 500 Cadets including 327 from 8 Districts of Arunachal and 52 girl cadets from Assam participated with full josh and enthusiasm. Cadets came from remote places like Anini, Tutting, Yingkiong, Aalo, Daporijo, Basar, Tezu, Mebo and Pasighat. During the Camp cadets were trained in Drill, Rifle Drill, Field Craft, Tent Pitching, Bayonet Fighting, Leadership, Games & Sports, Literary activities, cultural activities. Cadets also participated in Tree Plantation, Swachhta Rally. Such was the zeal and vigour that cadets were marching and playing in rain, under sunlight; day or night. Many cadets were marching in sports/canvass shoes and spontaneously singing patriotic songs!

NCC is one of the premier organizations of our nation which grooms youth towards transforming them into responsible citizens. Formed in 1948, NCC is the largest uniformed youth organization with strength of about 15 Lakh Cadets. The motto of NCC is "Unity and Discipline".

The NCC aims at developing character, comradeship, discipline, a secular outlook, the spirit of adventure and ideals of selfless service amongst young citizens. It also aims at creating a pool of organized, trained and motivated youth with leadership qualities in all walks of life. The aim of NCC are; To Create a Human Resource of Organized, Trained and Motivated Youth; To Provide Leadership in all Walks of life and be Always Available for the Service of the Nation; To Provide a Suitable Environment to Motivate the Youth to Take Up a Career in the Armed Forces.

It is estimated that presently there are about 8000 NCC Cadets in Arunachal Pradesh. The NCC Units in Arunachal comprise of 22 AP (I) Company at Pasighat under Dibrugarh Group, 1 AP Battalion Naharlagun &

2 AP Battalion Tawang (New Raising) under Tezpur Group. Presently NCC is predominantly offered to Govt schools and colleges.

NCC grooms the youth in fundamental values like discipline, teammanship, espirit-de-corps, leadership qualities, patriotism etc. These are steps towards making them responsible citizens of the nation. To imbibe these important values, some countries have compulsory military service like Singapore, Israel, Austria etc.

Youth trained and groomed by NCC are unlikely to be bad mannered, unruly, are unlikely to engage in arson, robbery, violence. NCC Cadets are likely to stay away from addictions like drugs, alcohol, smoking etc.

Don't we want to have disciplined, well behaved youth? Don't we want to have smart, obedient youth who are future leaders? With such an important contribution towards nation building, question arises why NCC should not be compulsory for all students for at least few years? It would be a good beginning to offer NCC to Private Schools also and maybe make NCC compulsory to all students from Class VI to Class VIII. Any takers?

9

ATMANIRBHAR ARUNACHAL

Economic Growth Drivers...!

Hamara Arunachal...the largest state in the north east, is also one of the least developed states of the country. As per Arunachal Pradesh Annual Planning document of 2011-12, the poverty level is much higher than the national average. Arunachal Pradesh is one of the Special Category States and is largely dependent on Central Assistance for Plan investment. As per the same document, Arunachal Pradesh continues to remain poorest of the poor State with inadequate basic infrastructure and low economic growth. The State is lagging far behind even in comparison to other North Eastern States in most of the indices of socio-economic development. Despite being rich in natural resources, the State is not in a position to harness its vast potential like hydropower, tourism, horticulture etc. The unemployment figures for Arunachal are also the second highest in the country!

Towards making Arunachal Pradesh into a better developed state, the following Economic Growth Drivers may be considered.

The **First Growth Driver is Roadways**. As per the same document, the State has the lowest road development index in the country with road density of 25.16 Km per 100 sq. km only. Even in comparison to the North Eastern Region, the State comes at the bottom of the rung. The first priority should be Two Lane All Weather Roads connecting the Capital with all District Headquarters and connecting District Headquarters to the supporting towns of Assam. Thereafter these roads can be extended to connect other towns and villages. Good roads will ensure faster travel time for passengers, goods, heavy equipment and products. Good roads will reduce losses of products/goods due to spillage and boost tourism. Trans Arunachal Highway is a good beginning and needs to be expedited.

The **Second Growth Driver is Electricity**. The power scenario in the state is erratic with frequent load shedding and very low voltage. As per the same planning document, the power requirement for the state is about 110 MW only. However this is also not being met despite the huge hydropower potential. The Govt notified Industrial Estates are without access to Three Phase Electricity. This is forcing the very few industries to run on generators. Availability of stabilised 24 X 7 electricity will lead to higher productivity due to increased man hours and efficiency. More industries will open up due to reduction in capital investment costs, reduction in production costs leading to competitive pricing of products. Cold Storages can open up the food processing and fruit industry. Uninterrupted electricity will also allow students to study and perform better.

The **Third Growth Driver is Bureaucracy**. Streamlined, simplified and clearly laid down laws, policies and time bound implementation will lead to efficient fructification of schemes and projects. Efficient administration will lead to expedited implementation of projects due to less paper work, faster clearances, less pre operative expenses and thus invite more investments in the state. Today there are more policies, more paper work and less investments in the state.

The **Fourth Growth Driver is Human Resources**. Law/ rule/ policy framers, administrators/ facilitators/ inspectors, policy/ scheme/ project implementers and workers are all human beings. Administration, policies, laws, schemes and implemented work are as good as the people. If people are sincere, hard working, disciplined and possess high integrity; administration, policies, laws, schemes and implemented work will be of a high order and the state will develop automatically. Human resources are the most important asset of any nation or state. Good human beings are a result of good educational system and a healthy society which lives by the values of integrity, discipline, hard work etc.

Of course there are many more Growth Drivers. However, for a start, if we begin focussing and rigorously implementing the growth drivers described above, Arunachal will take off on the path towards development in the next few years!

Don't we want to see Arunachal as one of the most developed states on North East India...if not India?

LET US MAKE IN ARUNACHAL...!

Who hasn't heard of *Samsung, Nokia, LG, Sony, Suzuki, Nike, Adidas, Vodafone, Xerox, Google, Facebook*? We proudly cruise on the highways in SUVs/Cars like *Honda CRV, Hyundai Creta, Toyota Fortuner* or *Nissan Terrano*. Similarly we enjoy the power and manoeuvrability of *Kawasaki, Yamaha* bikes. We see our popular TV shows on *Sony, LG, Samsung* TVs.

Did you know that *Honda, Toyota, Sony, Suzuki, Mitsubishi, Kawasaki, Yamaha* are all names of Japanese persons? Likewise *Canon, Nissan, Nikon, Akai, Sharp* are Japanese companies.

Mercedes, Renault, Volkswagen, Skoda, Audi, Adidas, Vodafone are European. *Samsung, Hyundai, Daewoo, LG* are all South Korean companies. *Ford, Chevrolet, Xerox, Google, Facebook, Microsoft, Nike, Reebok, KFC* are American companies. *Lenovo, Xiaomi, Huawei, Alibaba* are Chinese companies.

Famous Indian names like *Tata, Mahindra, Bajaj, Birla, Godrej* are commonly associated with vehicles, bikes, home furnitures, FMCG, Hotels etc.

Arunachal was declared a Union Territory in 1972 and became a State in 1987. Some older towns of Arunachal have conducted centenary celebrations. The first few schools and colleges of the state have conducted or nearing golden jubilee celebrations. 48 Years after becoming a Union Territory, we cannot claim to be a fresher. We have some experience below our belts!

However, almost all items bought in our state are made outside the state. Basic items like paper, pencil, pen, clothes, plates, glasses etc are imported from outside the state. Even bread, fish, vegetables are imported!! Even though we have sufficient bamboo, we import paper...even with sufficient fresh water, we import bottled water...despite harvesting large amounts of fresh orange, kiwi, pineapple etc we import fruits and fruit juice!

Products are imported from outside the state due to lack of manufacturing industries in the state. Lack of stable electricity, lack of infrastructure like good roads, railways etc, lack of single window licensing clearance, lengthy clearance process etc results in lack of industries in the state.

Slowly but surely things are changing for the better in our state also. Industrial Policies are being streamlined, clearances are being hastened up and incentives are being introduced for entrepreneurs. People are realising that there are limited government jobs. With the absence of major MNCs, Public Sector Undertakings, the only way to create jobs is through the manufacturing and services sector. The State Govt need to support these new industries in the state with preferential buying and preferential pricing policies.

In our lifetime, can we dream to talk on a *Perme* or *Dulom* mobile? Can we dream to watch our favourite programme on a *Nabam* or *Tshering* TV? Can we drive on a *Ete* or *Namchoom* bike? Can we write with a *Mena* or *Mosang* pen?

Someday...maybe...!!!

Lets Do Ourselves...!

A typical sight in all towns of Arunachal Pradesh is that almost all shops are manned by non natives. Grocery stores, readymade garment shops, gift shops, stationary shops, shoe shops are all manned by non natives. Chemists, hardware shops, motor spare parts shops are also manned by non natives. Fruit shops, vegetable shops, meat shops are also manned by non natives. Staff of hotels and restaurants are also mostly non natives.

Most major dealerships/ distributorships are with non natives. Wholesale supply of vegetables, fruits, eggs, poultry, fish, potato etc are controlled by non natives.

There are a few rare exceptions. A few natives are stepping into few fields like mobile networks, vehicle dealership etc. Local vegetables, some meat shops are slowly being manned by natives. In localised areas, very few small grocery shops/ gift shops are gradually being manned by natives.

Most skilled personnel like mechanics, electricians, plumbers, construction mishtries, barbers are also non natives. To build houses, to build boundary walls/ fences, to repair cycles,

motorcycles, scooties, cars, trucks, buses, autos, TVs, refrigerators, dish TV sets etc we rely on non natives.

In most cases, the licences are with natives, but the ventures are being managed/run by non natives. That means the real skill or learning or managing of the venture is by the non natives. That also means that the majority profit is being made by them.

So what could be the repercussions? Every time we pay for groceries, gifts, clothes, fish, eggs etc majority of the payments are channelized back to their home states/ home towns. Every time we pay for services like mishtries, electricians, plumbers, mechanics etc a major portion of the fees paid by us are sent back to respective home states/ home towns. Many of them have become rich and have invested most of the money outside our state.

If we ourselves start manning shops, start working as mishtries, electricians, plumbers, mechanics etc, the money paid for items/ services would remain circulated inside the state. This money can directly contribute to the development of the state.

With development, many new projects/ ventures are starting up in the state. There is an increasing demand for qualified professionals like Chartered Accountants, Architects, Bank Empanelled Lawyers, Certified Valuators etc. It is high time some natives start taking up these jobs.

We must realise that instead of remaining unemployed, it is better to start doing all kinds of jobs ourselves. There are many free lance electricians, mishtries, etc who are earning decent money by working in new houses, buildings and projects. Many of our youth may lead decent and comfortable lives by gradually taking over these roles.

To develop as a robust and economically self reliant society, we should inculcate dignity of labour and DO IT OURSELVES!

PROMOTE & SUPPORT LOCAL PRODUCTS

A conversation with a former broiler chicken farmer of our state revealed that he gave up broiler farming after trying for few years. On further enquiry he revealed that local broiler pricing could not compete with the prices of broilers imported from other states. Amongst the many reasons for failure was non availability of cheap skilled labour, expensive broiler feed, cartelisation by established big players outside the state, lack of supportive local policies etc.

In another case, the entrepreneur of a locally set up water bottling plant was called as a resource person by a local college. The irony was that the water bottles served in the function was from *Kinley* brand of Coca Cola Company of USA! Couldn't the college authorities be sensitive enough to use a local brand of bottled water? As local citizens, shouldn't we all promote local brands?

Similar stories can be experienced in the industries sector, textiles and handicrafts sector, farming sector, fish farming sector, horticulture etc. It is extremely difficult for local products to compete with products from outside the state.

The question is how do the Govt ensure that local products are supported and promoted? How does the Govt ensure that a level playing field is provided to local products vís-a-vís products imported from outside the state which are manufactured and aggressively marketed by established big players?

Some solutions may involve some combinations of the following steps. ***Step 1:*** To ensure that all Govt departments compulsorily procure local products if manufactured and available within the state. This policy of Preferential Buying and Preferential Pricing already exists in our state, however many Govt departments do not follow this policy! Many Govt departments are still using middlemen to import products from outside the state!!

Step 2: Introduce a price subsidy on locally produced items for the initial 4-5 years. **Step 3:** Introduce tax subsidies, transport subsidies, power subsidies to local manufacturers, farmers etc. This would reduce the manufacturing cost of local items to bring them at par with products produced outside the state.

Should mega stores like Vishal Mega Mart, Reliance Trends etc be allowed to sell Rice from Punjab, Dal from UP, Garments from Ludhiana etc at prices below the prevalent local prices freely? One way maybe is to ensure that these mega stores compulsorily procure 30 % of its products from local manufacturers.

Indian freedom struggle started with Swaraj. Slogans like Be Indian, Buy Indian; boycott Chinese products are propagated. In the same line, lesser developed states must promote and support local manufacturers and farmers by buying and using local products. The ideal support is when local population including local officers, local organisations, local NGOs, student groups etc instinctively buy and use local products.

If local industries, local farmers, fish farmers, horticulture farmers etc blossom large employment will be generated; the economy will be boosted and dependence on central grants would reduce.

Are Arunachalese ready to promote and support local products?

Industrial Revolution in Arunachal Pradesh & North East

North East India and Arunachal Pradesh have negligible industries as compared to rest of India. Since industrial production is minimal, most products are imported from mainland India. How long will North East & Arunachal be dependent on other states?

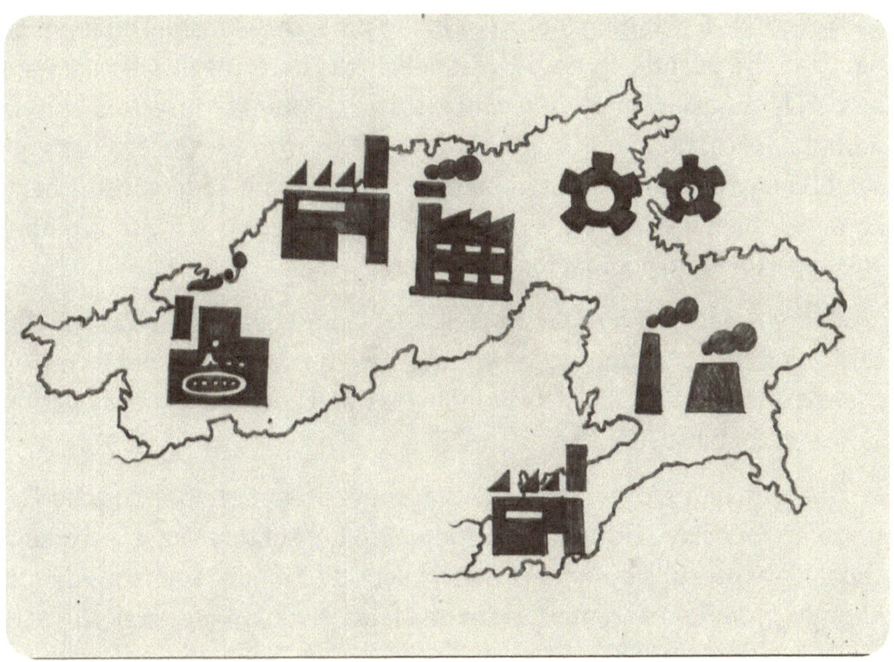

Lack of industries is further leading to less employment opportunities in the private sector and therefore growing unemployment amongst the youth. World over the private sector employs more people compared to the Govt sector. Unemployment leads to social problems like drug addiction, alcoholism, arson & theft, terrorism etc. The panacea to most of these social problems is by providing gainful employment.

North East & Arunachal are rich in raw materials like Oil, Gas, Iron Ore, Coal, Limestone, Dolomite, Tea, Wood, Bamboo, Oranges, Kiwi, Apples, Pineapple, Betel Nut etc. Oil, Coal, Iron Ore, Limestone, Coal are directly related to production of POL, Gas, Iron & Steel, Cement etc. Wood and Bamboo are linked to Furniture industry, artefacts, Paper Industry, toothpicks, matchbox, chopsticks, Agarbatti etc. Fruits are directly linked to Juice industry, Jams, Pickles, wine industry, Supari, Paan Masala etc. Even then there are negligible industries!

What are the ways to increase industries in North East & Arunachal? The primary requirement is willingness to set up and boost industries by the local state govts. Once the will is there the state should simplify procedures and processes for starting industries in the state. The industrial policy must be suited and oriented for easy investment in the state. The first requirement is a Truly Single Window Clearance system. Potential investors should submit application and documents to ONE Department. Once submitted, all necessary clearances should be obtained from this single department. Presently there are hundreds of windows and investors have to run from one department to another for clearances.

There is need for a separate dedicated Govt Agency to look after this entire process to setting up new industries. This agency should simplify and expedite setting up of new industries and promoting newly set up industries for initial 5-7 years.

Then there are other important incentives for starting industries like Transport Subsidy, Electricity Subsidy, Capital Subsidy/Grants, Working Capital interest subsidy, Project Report subsidy, Stamp Paper subsidy etc. Another important incentive is grant of Tax Holiday for initial 10 years like being done for SEZs. These subsidies/grants will help local products compete with products from big manufacturing companies of mainland India.

Other incentives are promotional policies like Preferential Buying and Preferential Pricing. It must be compulsory for all Govt departments to procure products from local manufacturers only. Infrastructure requirements include 24 X 7 Stabilised 3 Phase Electricity in all industrial estates, water supply, good road/rail/Air connectivity.

More industries will provide employment to local people, boost local enterprises like hotels/restaurants, rent houses, taxi/autos, banking, transport and contribute to economy of the region. Increased employment to youth will lead to more peace & stability in society. Any takers for an Industrial Revolution in Arunachal & North East?

CHANDRAYAAN: VOYAGE TO 'POLO'...!

After a successful launch on 22 July 2019, Chandrayaan-2 is presently orbiting the Moon and is planned to land *Vikram* Lander near the South Pole of the Moon on 07 September 2019. This would be India's second mission to the Moon after the partial success of Chandrayaan-1 during 2008-2009 during which a Moon Impact Probe impacted the Moon's surface in a controlled manner near the Moon's South Pole helping in collection of crucial data. Chandrayaan-1 orbited the Moon for almost one year before all signals were lost.

India is the fourth country in the world to successfully land on the Moon after USA, Russia and China. Readers are aware that USA successfully landed many astronauts on the Moon with Neil Armstrong being the first man to step on the moon on 20 July 1969. It has been a challenge to the scientific world to land and explore the Moon. Presently NASA is planning unmanned and manned missions to Mars!

Chandrayaan-2 was successfully launched from Sriharikota (Andhra Pradesh) by a Geosynchronous Satellite Launch Vehicle (GSLV Mk III). It consists of a Lunar Orbiter, *Vikram* lander, and a Lunar Rover named *Pragyan*, all made in India. The lander and the rover will land on the near side of the Moon on 07 September 2019. The wheeled *Pragyan* rover will move on the lunar surface and will perform on-site chemical analysis for 14 days (one lunar day). It can relay data to Earth through the Chandrayaan-2 orbiter and lander, which were launched together. The Lunar Orbiter will perform its mission for one year in a lunar orbit of 100 × 100 km.

After successful launch, Chandrayaan-2 orbited Earth with each orbit increasing in size to gradually exit Earth's gravity. It carried out precise manoeuvres to exit Earth's gravity and enter lunar orbit after the fifth Earth orbit. After entering Lunar Orbit, Chandrayaan will gradually decrease orbit size to reach a height for insertion of the *Vikram* Lander. Presently Chandrayaan-2 has completed the second lunar orbit.

The *Vikram* Lander will exit the lunar orbiter and carry out a 15 minutes descent to carry out a soft landing on the moon's surface. After landing, the *Pragyan* rover will exit the *Vikram* lander and explore the moon's surface for 14 Days (One Lunar Day). The lunar orbiter, *Vikram* Lander and *Pragyan* Rover are all carrying sophisticated cameras and sensors to transmit back collected data for detailed analysis.

All Indians and many people all over the world are excitedly awaiting the Moon landing on 07 September 2019. The event would be a successful technology demonstrator of India's progress in Space Technology. It would also help in gathering critical data for further exploration in space.

In many ways, it would be a major event for many Arunachalese also! Many Arunachalese worship and follow Donyi Polo; Polo stands for the Moon! That means humans are landing on Polo!!

10

ARUNACHAL SHINING

ARUNACHAL SHINING!

The last few months/years have seen many critical milestones being accomplished in Arunachal Pradesh. Most of these critical milestones have been achieved in the field of education and infrastructure.

In the education sector, the major milestone is the commencement of the First Medical College of the state, TRIHMS from this academic session. The inauguration of the much awaited Medical College in Arunachal Pradesh will allow specialist medical care in our remote state and open up vacancies for more Arunachali students to become doctors. In the long run this will reduce the dependency on Assam/NEIGRIHMS and Delhi/Chennai etc for medical treatment of Arunachali patients. A medical college was planned in Pasighat about 15-20 years ago but was shelved due to local politics!

The other major achievement is the commencement of the First Sainik School of Arunachal Pradesh at Niglok near Pasighat from this academic session on 27 August 2018. The much touted and much awaited Sainik School will allow Arunachali students to get quality education under discipline and military training. Sainik School will allow many Arunachali students to become Military Pilots, Army and Naval Officers.

The other major milestones include the re-commencement of commercial flights from Pasighat. This is enabling commuters from nearby areas to fly directly to Guwahati/Kolkata mitigating the irritating Assam Bandhs. The other major achievements are the inauguration of India's longest bridge, the 9.15 km Sadiya bridge connecting Dibrugarh/Tinsukia to Roing/Tezu and the 6.5 km bridge connecting Roing and Dambuk. The bridge connecting Roing and Dambuk is a lifeline to citizens of Dambuk area which was always cut off from rest of the state during summer months. Another major achievement is the inauguration of India's longest road-cum-rail bridge over Bogibeel connecting Dibrugarh with northern bank areas like, Pasighat, Aalo, Daporijo etc.

There are few more critical milestones planned to be inaugurated in the next few months/years like the commissioning of 110 MW *Pare* and 600 MW *Kameng* Hydro Power projects. The mega project consisting of the 2000 MW Subansiri Hydro Power Project is also almost complete. If the Govt of Arunachal and Assam resolve few pending issues, this dam will make entire North East self sufficient in power generation and power availability! Other important pending milestones include re-commencement of commercial flights from Tezu, Ziro and Mechukha.

With the present State Govt and Central Govt pushing forward the development agenda, it is likely that these pending critical milestones will be accomplished at an early date. Similar push is required in the Industries and Health sectors also. These critical infrastructure and educational milestones will trigger economic development in the state; give a fillip to tourism and thus generate gainful employment to the youth of the state. At this rate the day is not far when the new slogan is 'Arunachal Shining'!!

BRIDGING STATES, DISTRICTS & COMMUNITIES..!

Recently the Defence Minister of India Rajnath Singh inaugurated the strategically important Sisar or Sisseri bridge on 15 November 2019. The bridge connects Dambuk in Lower Dibang Valley district and Pasighat in East Siang district of Arunachal Pradesh. The 200 m long bridge has been constructed by Project Brahmank of Border Roads Organisation. During the inauguration ceremony many speakers narrated that Dambuk was called 'Kaala Pani' in reference to the famous Cellular Jail in Port Blair of Andaman group of islands since it was regularly cut-off from all sides every summer by the rampaging waters of the Sisseri and Dibang rivers. The Sisseri bridge would ensure all weather connectivity to & from Dambuk.

Recently three more strategically and economically important bridges were also commissioned in the region i.e. the 6.5 km Bomjir bridge connecting Roing/Tezu with Dambuk, the 9.15 km long Bhupen Hazarika Setu (longest river bridge in India) connecting Tinsukia/Dhola of Assam with Roing/Tezu of Arunachal and the 4.95 km long Road cum Rail bridge connecting Dibrugarh/Tinsukia/Jorhat of Assam with northern bank of Brahmaputra including many districts of Arunachal Pradesh like East Siang, West Siang, Lower Siang, Upper Subansiri, Papumpare.

These key bridges have brought about a paradigm shift in terms of connectivity giving a boost to economics and business. These bridges have cut down travel time between places by nearly 5-6 hours. Citizens can travel from Namsai/Tezu/Roing to Itanagar in shorter time through Arunachal. Presently Orange, Valencia, Kiwi, Pineapple fruit farmers from Arunachal have easy access to the vast markets of Assam towns. Ginger, Cardamom farmers, bamboo/cane suppliers have access to the Assam markets. Similarly

Arunachalese have easy access to better items at cheaper rates from shops and wholesalers of Assam.

These bridges have strategic importance also. These bridges will allow quick mobilisation and deployment of military equipment and troops from deeper bases to forward areas. This would strengthen our security preparedness.

However the big jump has been in terms of connecting communities between states and districts. Every weekend, tourists & revellers from Dibrugarh, Tinsukia, Sibsagar, Jorhat travel for weekend trips to Tezu, Roing, Pasighat, Aalo, Malinithan etc to enjoy the pristine and beautiful hills/ valleys/ streams of Arunachal. Similarly, Arunachalese travel to Dibrugarh/ Tinsukia for shopping, business, for better medical care and for boarding flights to other cities. In fact some Arunachalese travel just to see a movie or enjoy a pizza! These frequent interactions between people from Assam & Arunachal would foster cultural relations and inter-community bonds.

These bridges allow enthusiasts to have breakfast in Assam, Lunch in Arunachal and return for Dinner and sleep in their homes in Assam! On the flip side, people from Assam have easy access to *Bamboo Shoot & Apong*...& Arunachalese have access to *Pitha & Gamusa!*

Arunachal of Our Dreams..!

Since NEFA days, Arunachal Pradesh has undergone enormous transformation. The population increased from 3.5 Lakhs in 1961 to about 13.8 Lakhs in 2011 census. The original 5 Districts has gone up to 28 Districts presently. Many new towns have come up and olden towns are on the verge of becoming cities. From only one college at Pasighat, there are now dozens of colleges and many Universities.

Today Arunachal has more roads, more electric lines, more schools, colleges, universities, more vehicles and also more Lakhpaties/Crorepaties! Today we have mobile/internet connectivity in most areas, Dish TVs, remotely operated TVs etc. Old Assam type buildings have given way to multi-storied RCC buildings. We have air conditioners to remain cool, refrigerators to preserve food and smart mobiles to do almost everything!

However, Arunachalese are dreaming for more. Though our state has progressed on many fronts, we are still lagging behind most states and nations in many parameters.

Arunchalese want more improvements in Roads, Electricity, Water Supply! We want better all weather roads connecting our towns and villages.

Better roads will reduce travel time between places and reduce maintenance cost of vehicles. Along with better roads, we require more railways and more airports for better flight connectivity. Better roads, railways and flight connectivity will promote tourism, industries and usher in development.

Citizens want Stabilised 24 X 7 Electricity supply without voltage fluctuations in all our towns and villages. Stabilised 24 X 7 Electricity supply will boost education, productivity, tourism and industries. Presently power supply is erratic with voltage fluctuations and too many breakdowns!

Arunachalese want better civic amenities like water supply, drainage and sanitation. Despite numerous rivers, there are many areas in the state without access to healthy drinking water. Better drainage, sanitation and waste management will lead to healthy lifestyle with lesser diseases.

Arunachalese want better schools, better colleges, better Universities and better quality education. There is need for better medical facilities/care for our citizens.

Arunachalese want more employment as there are many unemployed youth. More employment can be generated by more industries, tourism and service industries.

Arunachalese also want better governance; efficient and effective governance. Better governance will lead to more productivity, more development and enhance the living standards of common citizens. It will also lead to less pilferage of Govt funds!

Arunachalese also require better leaders, politicians and bureaucrats who have more integrity and less self service.

Arunachalese dream for better health, more happiness and a peaceful & stable society. Do you also desire Arunachal of our Dreams?

WHERE ARUNACHALESE DARE?

Since Arunachal Pradesh became a Union Territory in 1972, many Arunachalese have charted pioneering paths to succeed in varied fields. When most of the state was underdeveloped, without basic facilities like electricity, roads and communications with very few schools & colleges, these pioneers toiled and persevered to venture into previously unknown fields. Many of these pioneers had to walk for days to reach school and were the first in their families and villages to study in schools and colleges. Many had to travel to far flung places in North East and other cities of India for further education like graduation, medicine, engineering, law etc.

These trail blazing Arunachalese include Jomin Tayeng the First IAS officer, Dr Odang Lego the first Doctor, Daying Ering who was the First Union Minister, Chowkhamon Gohain the First MP, C Manpung the First Engineer, Yeshi Dorjee Thongchi the First Sahitya Akademi Winner.

This pioneering list includes Colonel Rimo Karbak the First Army Officer, Late Kuru Hassang the First Pilot, Shri Taru Talo the First Navy Officer, Shri Robin Hibu the First IPS officer. Major General Jarken Gamlin is the first to reach the coveted Major General rank.

Amongst the pioneering women are Late Omem Moyong Deori the First Padma awardee, Dr Beena Namchum Karbak the First Lady Doctor, Mamang Dai Sahitya Academi winner and Padma awardee, Indra Mallo first lady IAS officer, Tine Mena who was the First woman to climb Mt Everest, Lieutenant Colonel Ponung Doming the First lady Army officer, Late Binny Yanga Social Activist & Padma awardee.

Pioneers in sports include Indrajit Namchoom who was captain of Indian Football team, Gumpe Rime who played football at the national level, Tapi Mra the First to climb Mt Everest, Lhakpa Tshering the First to win Himalayan Car Rally, RK Mission School Aalo which was runners up in two Subroto Cups.

International achievers include Dr Alai Taggu, who has been made the Head of Department, Critical Care Medicine in multispecialty International Hospital in Dubai, United Arab Emirates and Nixon Bui a Denmark based entrepreneur who is making a mark in fashion and liquor internationally.

The First and only college in the state for many years was JN College Pasighat. NERIST was the First Engineering College. The First Medical college TRIHMS was opened last year only. There was a period when there was no University to award degrees. Presently there are many colleges & Universities in the state. One of the major contributors to Arunachal are Rama Krishna Mission Schools, Sharda Mission Schools and Vivekananda Kendra Vidyalayas. These schools have played a pioneering role in grooming and training our youth.

Then there was Hangpan Dada the First Ashok Chakra of the state. Presently there are many Kirti Chakra and other gallantry winners like Sena Medal, Arunachal Ratna.

Today Arunachal has Super Specialist doctors, scientists, top engineers, Professors, Doctorates, Top Lawyers and many more. Many young Arunachalese are doing well in Karate, Taekwondo, Weight Lifting and other sports. Talented young Arunachalese have participated in India's Got Talent, Voice of India, Indian Idol, Dance India Dance etc

Yet there are many more fields to be conquered by Arunachalese. We need more top Pilots, Astronauts, Chartered Accountants, Managers, Entrepreneurs, Progressive farmers, Sports persons etc. To be pioneers in different fields, one has to persevere and work hard to succeed.

By the way yours truly is the First from North East and Arunachal to Command a Sukhoi-30MKI Squadron! Any more Arunachalese willing to Dare?

ARUNCHAL MAANGE MORE..!

Arunachal Pradesh has come a long way since the NEFA days. The population increased from about 3.5 Lakhs in 1961 census to about 13.8 Lakhs in 2011 census. From the original 5 Districts we have increased to 28 Districts presently. Many new towns have come up and olden towns are on the verge of becoming cities. From only one college at Pasighat, there are now hundreds of colleges and many Universities.

Today Arunachal has more roads, more electric lines, more schools, colleges, universities, more vehicles, more education and also more Lakhpaties/Crorepaties! Today we have mobile/ internet connectivity in majority areas, satellite Dish TVs, remotely operated TVs etc. Old Assam type buildings have given way to multi-storied RCC buildings. We have air conditioners to remain cool, refrigerators to preserve food and smart mobiles to do almost everything!

However, can Arunachali citizens be satisfied? Though our state has progressed on many fronts, we are still lagging behind most states and nations in many parameters.

Arunchalese want better BIJLI, SADAK, PAANI and ROTI! We want better all weather roads; better roads connecting our towns and villages. Better roads will reduce travel time between places and reduce maintenance cost of vehicles. Along with better roads, we require more railways and more flight connectivity. Better roads, railways and flight connectivity will promote tourism, industries and usher in development.

Citizens want Stabilised 24 X 7 Electricity supply without voltage fluctuations in all our towns and villages. Stabilised 24 X 7 Electricity supply will boost education, productivity, tourism and industries. Presently power supply is erratic with voltage fluctuations and too many breakdowns!

Arunachalese want better civic amenities like water supply, drainage and sanitation. Despite numerous rivers, there are many areas in the state without access to healthy drinking water. Better drainage, sanitation and waste management will lead to healthy lifestyle with lesser diseases.

Arunachalese want better schools, better colleges and better Universities. There is need for better medical facilities/care for our citizens.

Arunachalese want more employment as there are many unemployed youth. More employment can be generated by more industries, tourism and service industries.

Arunachalese also want better governance; efficient and effective governance. Better governance will lead to more productivity, more development and enhance the living standards of common citizens. It will also lead to less pilferage of Govt funds!

Arunachalese also require better leaders, politicians and bureaucrats who have more integrity and less self service.

The list is almost endless. ARUNACHAL MAANGE MORE!!

GLOSSARY

Abu	Father
Apong	Local Rice Beer
Bamboo Shoot	Young, edible bamboo shoots
Bandh	Lock downs of certain area or districts
Bhang	Local Cannabis preparation
BIJLI, SADAK, PAANI and ROTI	Electricity, Road, Water & Bread
Bindass	Carefree, Relaxed
Dao	Local Small Sword carried by locals
'Dao Dekha Hai…?'	Seen my Sword?
Dar Ke Aage Jeet Hain	Beyond fear lies victory
Donyi Polo	Local deities Sun & Moon
Gaon Bura	Village Headman
Gitti/Ballu	Stone & Sand
Hamara	Our, Mine
Harings	Local word for outsiders
Housie	Local name for Tambola game
Indi-Chini Bhai-Bhai	India-China Brothers
Jelebis, Pakoras and Mala Rotis	Local sweets and snacks
'Kaat Dunga'	Will Cut/Chop you
Kebangs/Kebaa/Mels	Local Community Meetings

Khushi Khushi	Everyone's free will
Kutcha	Raw, Temporary
Kyonki	Because
Lakhpaties/Crorepaties	Millionaires, Billionaires
Maange	Demand or Want in Hindi
Maar Dunga'	Will Hit/Kill you
Mishtries	Construction workers
Mithun	Local sacred animal *Bos Frontalis*
NEFA	North East Frontier Agency
Paan	Leaves of Betel Plant
Paan ghumties	Small shops selling Paan
Pitha & Gamusa!	Assamese rice cake & hand towel
Prabhat Pheris	Morning march by students, youth
Saheed	Martyr
Strilling and *Pulling*	Feminine & Masculine genders
Supari, Paan Masala	Dried Areca nut & Paan mixture
Swacchta	Cleanliness

www.ingramcontent.com/pod-product-compliance
Lightning Source LLC
Chambersburg PA
CBHW051251250726
48656CB00004B/1244